JAZZ DIDN'T JUST HAPPEN.
LOUIS ARMSTRONG MADE IT HAPPEN.

MEET SATCHMO
A MUSIC IMMORTAL

He found his life's passion when he was living in the Home for Colored Waifs in his hometown of New Orleans and began playing a battered old trumpet. Soon he was playing those sweet, often salty, notes in every funeral parade, every honky-tonk and "parlor" in New Orleans' famed Storyville.

But New Orleans soon proved to be too small a pond for this king of jazz. Satchmo headed north, first to Chicago, where the legend began to grow, then on to Harlem where his fame mushroomed. From there he conquered the world with his music.

Women problems, bad managegent, traditional prejudice and criticism from his own people plagued the father of jazz for many years. But he survived, met his challenges with characteristic forthrightness, and always came out on top.

Brilliant writing by author Robert Hoskins makes this must-read book a delightful entertainment. His word pictures of Satchmo the man, of New Orleans and Harlem are fascinating, priceless. This is a big book. You'll enjoy the experience.

LOUIS ARMSTRONG

BIOGRAPHY OF A MUSICIAN

BY ROBERT HOSKINS

AN ORIGINAL HOLLOWAY HOUSE EDITION

HOLLOWAY HOUSE PUBLISHING CO.
LOS ANGELES, CALIFORNIA

PUBLISHED BY
Holloway House Publishing Company
8060 Melrose Avenue
Los Angeles, California 90046

International Standard Book Number 0-87067-668-7
Printed in the United States of America
Cover illustration by Jesse Santos
Cover Design by Davidson Graphics

CONTENTS

1
"GOODBYE, POPS"

1

"Goodbye, Pops"

Thursday, July 8, 1971:

The sun rose over the tenements and high rise apartment complexes of Queens and Brooklyn at the start of what would prove to be the hottest day thus far of the year. It was already brutal, baking the pavement and turning thousands of tenement rooms and apartments into sweat boxes. Thousands had illegally spent the night in one or another of the great parks of the city, ignoring the midnight curfews. Other thousands flowed onto the burning concrete sidewalks, nightworkers on their way home and dayworkers pouring into the subways on their way to another uncomfortable day in Manhattan.

At 6 a.m. the overnight low was reached: a muggy 76 degrees. Humidity was uncomfortably high. The muggy air left dirt streaks across foreheads when brows were mopped with handerchiefs and turned collars of white shirts black. The demand for deodorants and antiperspirants soared. Yet those early riders were lucky. They found seats in the subway cars. Many of those starting from home an hour later would have to stand during the long ride from Jamaica Avenue or Pelham Parkway, from Flatbush and Yonkers.

Another typical miserable summer day in New York: yet this was not just another day for many of those headed into the city from the bedroom communities of New Jersey, Connecticut and Westchester County. Not all of them went straight to work. Some detoured, heading uptown to 66th Street and Park Avenue. There the crowds formed early, gathering outside the stately red brick walls of the Gothic Seventh Regimental Armory. They had come, those thousands and thousands more who took extra time on their lunch hours or changed their homeward route, to pay honor to one man, who lay in state within the Armory.

By 8 o'clock the temperature had climbed another degree, but it seemed much hotter to those hundreds already in the lines that stretched down Park Avenue. Controlled by police barricades, the mourners waited patiently while clothing wilted and feet arched from standing on the hot pavement. The doors would not open until 10 o'clock; by that time the temperature had climbed to 84 degrees. Still the people waited, patiently, filled with love and sorrow for the man in his coffin. For fifty years he had used his magic horn to spread joy over almost all of the world. It was only fitting that they sacrifice a few hours of time, a bit of comfort, to show Louis Armstrong just how much they loved him.

10 o'clock: the great entrance doors to the Armory

swung open on the stroke of the hour, and the crowd surged into the huge and ornate front hall. For many, this was the first time they had come to the old Armory, although it had been the scene of many social functions, of balls and public exhibitions, for most of its long life.

For the little people who had come this day, balls and public exhibitions were not in their normal social activities. There were no dignitaries here today; they would come tomorrow, to the funeral services at 1:00 o'clock at the Corona Congregational Church. The church, at 34th Avenue and 103rd Street in Corona, Queens, was only four blocks from the home Louis Armstrong had shared with Lucille, his fourth wife and his companion during the last twenty-nine years. Those who could not make it to the Armory or to the funeral could watch tomorrow's services on WPIX-TV, Channel 11, the television station of the New York Daily News. It would be the first funeral to be telecast live in New York City since the death of President John F. Kennedy.

Following the funeral, burial would be in Flushing Cemetery, also in Queens. The church would be crowded, hundreds of well-wishers forced to wait outside, on the street; many more were coming only to see the famous among the invited guests. Yesterday, the New York Times published the list of honorary pallbearers. Included were Governor Nelson Rockefeller of New York State, Mayor John V. Lindsay of New York City, and a galaxy of stars and the merely-famous from the world of show business and music.

Old friends were on the list, some coming thousands of miles to pay their last respects to the man known familiarly as Pops—the greatest of jazz. Bing Crosby and Ella Fitzgerald had been friends for more than forty years, since he first made music with them. In his early days, before he became known as a crooner—although it may seem incredible to those who did not know the Bing Crosby who got his start with Paul Whiteman's Rhythm Boys—he copied much of his style from Louis Armstrong's early recordings.

Close friends were coming as well: Duke Ellington and Dizzy Gillespie, Pearl Bailey and Count Basie, Harry James and Bobby Hackett. Guy Lombardo had been a dear friend for forty-five years, ever since the Royal Canadians first crossed the border to play in Chicago. Many were the nights Pops sat in with the Lombardo orchestra in those days, when they played on Cottage Grove; and later, when the sweetest music this side of heaven was heard echoing from the Steel Pier in Atlantic City.

In Louis Armstrong's mind, music was music. Call the style whatever you like, he said time and again that no other band could play a straight lead like the Lombardo orchestra and make it sound so good. At the Atlantic City gig, after half an hour the fans were ready to tear the place apart to show their appreciation.

Respected friends would be there tomorrow: Frank Sinatra and Ed Sullivan, Broadway columnist Earl Wilson and comedian Alan King. Television friends were coming: Johnny Carson and David Frost, Merv Griffin and Dick Cavett. Some of the honorary pallbearers had known Pops half a century; others only a few years. Every one of them, like America, had grown up with his music.

An honor guard of black boys and girls in crisp military uniforms had come from the Cadet Corps of Central Harlem and from the Drug and Bugle Corps of the 28th Police Precinct Athletic League. The youngsters stood by the simple gray steel coffin lined with white velvet, which rested beneath the grand wooden staircase of the Armory. The bier was banked with bunches of gladioluses and chrysanthemums, carnations and red roses.

As the mourners filed past the coffin there were tears in many of the eyes. Old women were among the first to come, among those who had waited the longest. Young executives appeared later, those who had extended their lunch hours. Little children who didn't know Pops at all were brought by their parents to pay homage to the giant of musical gaints. Among the latter were Cindy and Lisa, eight and nine-year-old daughters of Tommy Benford, who had been the drummer in Jelly Roll Morton's band during the early 1930s. Tommy Benford was one of the thousands of musicians who had known Pops since he first came to Chicago in 1922.

Young and old, white and black, they all came, to pause a moment, reading the plain gold plaque affixed to the silk lining of the raised coffin lid: *Louis Satchmo Armstrong*. That was all it said. Nothing more was needed. He was the King. Satchmo. Pops.

He was Louis Armstrong, the greatest horn player who ever came out of New Orleans. Born when jazz was still called ragtime, developing out of the enthusiasm of untrained street musicians, Pops followed the music up the mighty Mississippi to Chicago and then to New York. Along the way something happened: at first another horn blower—although recognized as one of the most talented—jazz soon became his music. Louis Armstrong became jazz.

An estimated twenty-five thousand mourners filed past the coffin during the twelve hours from 10 a.m. to 10 p.m. while the historic man of music lay in state in the historic old Armory. They saw him dressed in a navy blue suit, pink shirt and pink-and-silver figured tie with an immaculate starched handerchief in his left hand.

The heat and the humidity continued to climb, until at 5 p.m. the high for the day of 96 degrees was reached. That was only two degrees below the all-time record high for the day, set in 1937.

Only four months earlier Pops had played the last of many thousands of gigs in a career that started when he was a boy, before World War I came to America: two weeks at the Waldorf-Astoria's Empire Room. Some of his advisors tried to tell him not to do it, but nothing mattered to Pops except his horn and his music.

His last show was on March 13th, 1971. Two days later Louis Armstrong entered Beth Israel Hospital, suffering from heart failure and from liver and kidney disease. Small one-paragraph stories buried deep in the pages of the nation's leading newspapers announced his hospitalization, and again March 24th, small stories reported that his condition had worsened. A severe pulmonary infection set in. His doctors had to perform an emergency tracheotomy to let Pops keep on breathing. It was a close thing; he almost didn't make it that time.

Eight weeks later his indomitable constitution had recovered far enough to let Pops be released from the hospital, sent to the comfortable home in Corona to rest up from his ordeal. When old friends dropped by to say hello, his spirits seemed high. Pops talked of performing again, of concerts planned for the future. He had been forced to cancel out of the climactic program of the New Orleans Jazz and Heritage Festival in April, which was to have been a tribute to his life and music.

Old friend Kid Ory filled in for him. Pops had got his first real job in Ory's band when he was just a kid, replacing Joe King Oliver who had gone to Chicago. It was Kid Ory's first visit in fifty-two years to New Orleans, his hometown and the city where jazz was born.

Pops was the King now and had been for almost fifty years. He had tens of thousands of friends, young and old, old and new. Even those music experts who sometimes criticized Pops for his mugging and showmanship agreed that Louis Armstrong was the one man who had taken jazz from the raw and gutsy folk music of New Orleans funeral parades and honky-tonks and made it an authentic American art form. Some think jazz is the only native American music.

Pops died July 6, 1971, two days after his seventy-first birthday. In his seventy-one years of life he rose from the seamiest slums of New Orleans, which at the time of his birth and childhood was considered the most wide open sink of vice and iniquity in the United States, to play command performances before the crowned heads and royal houses of Europe. In his travels around the world Pops and his trumpet came to symbolize the United States to millions of people on almost every continent.

The story of his death made the front pages. In the next few days and weeks thousands of words were written about Louis Armstrong and his career, all laudatory. There was an immediate outpouring of condolences, from the most humble of the land to the most famous. Even the State Department issued a statement in gratitude for the many times Pops had acted as an international ambassador of good will: "His memory will be enshrined in the archives of effective international communications."

The words might have been too flowery for Pops, whose schooling stopped with the fifty grade; but he would have understood the sentiment. In the first six

weeks after his death his family received thirty-nine
letters and telegrams. In the weeks and months to come
memorial tributes and performances would be given all
over America.

But on this day, the last mourner to file into the
Armory was one of the simple people, one Jack Samuel,
of 165 West 180th Street, New York City. That is not
one the exclusive residential districts of the city. It is an
area of old homes and aging red brick apartments, not
very far away from the approaches to the George
Washington Bridge. Jack Samuel was not famous, but
he had come to show his love for Pops.

The family had requested that no music be played at
the Armory, but Jack Samuel had brought his cornet.
Officials tried to take the instrument away from him. A
vigorous argument, followed, but at last they gave in.
Jack Samuel was permitted to honor the dead man by
playing three choruses of the Civil War-inspired call for
lights out, "Taps."

There were few present who knew the words to the
bugle call, perhaps few who even knew that General
Alexander Butterfield, composer of "Taps" and
founder of the famous stagecoach line that rivaled Wells
Fargo in importance, had set words to his music. But
the words were apt:

> *Day is done*
> *Gone the sun*
> *From the earth*
> *From the hills,*
> *From the sky.*
> *Day is done,*
> *Gone the sun . . .*
> *Night is nigh.*

The plaintive notes of the music died.
The King was dead.

2
A SOUTHERN DOODLE DANDY

2
A Southern Doodle Dandy

The site where New Orleans was founded and became the cradle of jazz was first spotted in 1699 by the brothers Pierre and Jean Baptiste Le Moyne. Leaders of a party of Frenchmen, the brothers saw a vista of flat land nestled inside a deep curve of the river. An Indian passage cut through the neck of land to a narrow lake behind the river, giving a back way into the Gulf.

Jean Baptiste Le Moyne, Sieur de Bienville, never forgot that stretch of the river, which was almost the only reasonable dry area along the banks of the Mississippi. The first French settlements were made along the sandy shores of the Gulf, but Bienville tried a number of times to receive permission to found settlements further upstream. At last, in 1718, he was allowed to establish La Nouvelle Orleans one hundred and ten miles up the river. The settlement was named for the profligate Duc d'Orleans, regent for the young Louis XV.

The location was not popular with the settlers brought in by Bienville, for the new town was almost entirely surrounded by water, swamps and marshes. The latter began a scant ten blocks back from the river. The town prospered, however, and after fifty years ownership was transferred to the Spanish King Carlos III by his royal Bourbon cousin, the same Louis XV.

In 1803, Spain gave New Orleans back to France, to Napoleon. The French of the city had been outraged by the first transfer and gave the new Spanish governor a great deal of trouble. In time, however, the Spanish assimilated. The descendants of both intermarried, creating the famous Creole culture.

Then Napolean outraged everyone, French and Spanish alike, by selling Louisiana to the infant United States.

Daniel Louis Armstrong—or perhaps Louis Daniel, or just Louis; the birth records have been lost, and there has been dispute over the right version of his name—was born in New Orleans ninety-seven years after it became United States property. His parents were Mary Ann nee Albert and Willie Armstrong.

In a 1969 interview with the New York Times, Satchmo said: "I was a southern Doodle Dandy, born on the 4th of July. My mother, Mary Ann—we called her Mayann—was living in a two-room shack in James Alley, in the Back O' Town *sic* colored section of New Orleans. It was a tough block—all them hustlers and their pimps and their gamblers and their knives—between Gravier and Perdido Streets."

Much of Louis Armstrong's early life remains in dispute, although he published two books about himself and his music: *Swing That Music* and *My Life in New Orleans.* About half of the sources say that he was born on Jane Alley, but Satchmo insisted to his death that it was James Alley.

Apparently no one has bothered checking the source. The New Orleans City Directory for 1913, the earliest edition I have been able to locate, lists James Street and Jane Alley; but there is no James Alley. Further, Max Jones, in his 1971 *Louis,* published a photograph of a street sign clearly marked 'Jane Alley' and 'Perdido.' *Louis* was published after Armstrong's death, but Jones had been in correspondence with Satchmo while the book was being written. Thus it would appear that Louis' memory frequently failed him.

In a letter to Jones, who lived in England, Louis said that the day of his birth was "a blasting Fourth of July, my mother called it, that I came into the world and they named me the firecracker baby."

The French and the Spanish called all of the Americans of their time "Kaintucks,' because most of the river boatmen came from Kentucky. It was not a friendly phrase, and the Creoles tried to ostracize the newcomers, both socially and from business. Miffed, the Americans established their own section of town on the high ground south of the *Vieux Carre,* the old French Quarter. The section claimed by the upstarts became Uptown. Downtown, beyond the *Vieux Carre,* to the north, was low to the river and subject to frequent floodings. As the city expanded, this became the commercial district. The first settlements in the swamp area weren't made until the 1830s.

By the turn of the century this area known as "back of the Quarter," had become a slum with shacks and decrepit old public buildings such as Funky Butt Hall, a

dance hall with cracks in the walls so large the youngsters of the area could listen to the bands play for the
popular Saturday night dances.

It was at Funky Butt Hall that Louis first heard
Buddy Bolden, considered the king of the early jazz
musicians. Some have claimed that he learned his style
of playing from Bolden, but Bolden suffered a nervous
breakdown during a 1907 funeral parade and spent the
rest of his life in an asylum. It was seven years later that
Louis Armstrong learned to play the cornet, although
even this has been disputed. In later years Bunk Johnson, another of the great musicians of that time,
claimed to have taught the young Louis while the boy
hung around the honky-tonks where Johnson played.

Satchmo denied this emphatically. According to him,
Johnson had no time for the youngsters of the district at
all. And with the example of literally scores of noted
trumpet and cornet players around him during his boy-
hood, it seems doubtful he would have styled himself
after someone not heard since he was seven years old.

The streets back of the Quarter were unpaved, muddy
during the rainy season. James (or Jane) Alley was in
the center of an area called The Battlefield, named for
the constant fighting in the bars and dance halls and
even in the streets. Shootings and knifings were common, and most of the men carried their straight razors
at all times. Mayann later told Louis that the night he
was born, two men were killed in a knife fight outside
their small house.

The block between Gravier and Perdido was one of
the most crowded in the city with its gamblers, its pimps
and prostitutes, its thieves, hustlers, a perhaps-surpris-
ing number of God-fearing churchgoers and an inex-
haustible supply of children. The district was equally

crowded with saloons, bars and honky-tonks.

At the time of Louis' birth, Mayann and Willie lived with Willie's mother, Mrs. Josephine Armstrong. Although, like everything else in the early years in his life, even this has been disputed. However, wherever possible I have accepted Satchmo's own version of his early life.

The domestic situation was not happy. Willie Armstrong was a handsome man who had an eye for the pretty girls. His greatest pride in later life was in dressing up in his best formal clothing and stepping out as Grand Marshall of the Elks' Club parades.

Mayann and Willie quarreled frequently, until finally Mayann moved out, to a place at Liberty and Perdido Streets. It was a district of cheap prostitutes, who didn't make as much money as the girls who worked in Storyville, the famous red light district of the city. The latter was named for Alderman Sidney Story, one of the most respected businessmen and politicians of the city. He returned from an 1897 trip to Europe to suggest that New Orleans control the problems of prostitution by limiting it to a single district. To his great distress, the district was soon given his name, and for years he tried to live down the shame.

If Mayann did any hustling with the girls of the district, she never let her children know it. When Louis rejoined her, a few years later, there were a constant stream of "stepfathers" moving through the little house, which was in the backyard of a bigger place. Mayann finally settled down with one man when she got religion, some time between 1912 and 1915.

A short time later, after Mayann left her husband and her son, Willie Armstrong moved out as well, leaving Louis to the care of his grandmother, Josephine. A year later Willie went to work in a turpentine factory in the district, stoking furnaces. He stayed there for the rest of his life, until his death in 1933. In time, Willie Armstrong rose to a position of some authority in the company, hiring and firing the black laborers who worked under him.

According to his own version of events, several years were to pass before Louis saw either of his parents again, although both Mayann and Willie lived only a short distance away. After two years of separation, Willie left his current woman and returned to Mayann. The result of the temporary reconciliation was a girl, Beatrice, later nicknamed Mama Lucy. Louis was five before he saw his sister for the first time.

The two primary influences on the small boy were his grandmother, Josephine, and his great-grandmother; the latter isn't named in any of the available source material, although Louis spoke fondly of her. The old lady lived to be ninety, after having been born in slavery. Mayann and Willie were both young when their son was born, but it seems likely that Josephine Armstrong had also been born in slavery.

Josephine supported the boy and herself by taking washing and ironing, while Mayann was usually employed as a cook to one or another white family. When Louis grew big enough to help Josephine deliver the baskets of clothes, she gave him a nickel. With that much money in his pocket, the boy felt positively rich.

Josephine Armstrong was strict, although in a haphazard sort of way. A large chinaberry tree grew in the yard of her house, and when she felt Louis had done something that merited punishment, she sent him to cut a switch off the tree. He always returned with the smallest switch he could find, which sometimes made her laugh and relent. Other times, however, her ire increased, and she proceeded to whip Louis for every sin, large and small, committed since the last punishment. Later, when he moved back to his mother, Mayann adopted the same system.

As a small boy, Louis was given a number of nicknames. Besides Satchmo, one that stuck was Dippermouth, later shortened to just Dipper, and with so much in his life, there is a great deal of dispute about the derivation of Satchmo. According to Louis himself, Percy Mathison Brooks, editor of the English music journal, the *Melody Maker*, greeted him with the name when he first stepped ashore in that country in 1932. According to Max Jones, Louis spoke to his trumpet, using "Watch it, Satchelmouth," on the 1930 recording of *You're Driving Me Crazy*.

There was no mention of the name in print before his visit to England, but the August issue of *Melody Maker* made several references to his trumpet, "Satch-Mo." Jones guessed that in preparing copy, somebody gave it the abbreviation to impart a touch of black dialect. Henri Selmer's ad in that August issue stated: 'Satch-Mo' is a Selmer "Challenger" Trumpet. A feature story in the issue was "England's Welcome to Louis Armstrong," illustrated with cartoons; one of the latter had Louis saying to his horn, "Speak to 'em, Satch'-mo'." The following month, the maker of musical instruments, Selmer, had switched the name from the instrument and applied it to the man.

Louis always claimed that Percy Brooks was responsible for the name. Max Jones says not. Edgar Jackson, also on the staff of *Melody Maker*, told him: [I] . . . had for some time known Louis as Satchmo from having heard him called that in 1928 by the American musicians in Fred Elizalde's dance orchestra at the Savoy . . . it will probably never be known who thought it up.''

There were always plenty of children to play in the district, although there were few, if any, paved streets. When Louis grew large enough, Josephine made him attend school regularly, and go to church and Sunday School as well. It was in the latter two institutions that he learned to sing along with the congregations and thus received his first exposure to music as something that he could make himself.

As a boy, Louis sang in a clear high tenor. In later life, his voice was described as ''a piece of sandpaper calling to its mate.'' Yet his singing was as much a part of his success as his trumpet playing. Whenever and wherever Louis Armstrong appeared, his magical presence lit up auditoriums.

From the time that New Orleans came into possession of the United States, the city became a melting pot of diverse cultures. The strongest, of course, was the Creole. The city early developed its own distinctive style of living and architecture, although most of the buildings in the French Quarter actually owe their design to the Spanish occupation. The original city had been nearly wiped out in a series of disastrous fires.

Because of the high water table, the buildings were built on high foundations; there were no such things as cellars. During the early days, before drainage projects lowered the water table somewhat, coffins had holes drilled into the bottom to let the water pour in when the casket was set into the grave. Two strong, heavy men stood on the coffin to weigh it down while the grave was filled. Even then, when the ground became saturated during the rainy season, the coffins sometimes floated to the surface. Most burials, at least for the well-to-do, were above ground in crypts into brick walls. This is still the preferred method today.

When the United States was first opened west of the Cumberland Mountains, New Orleans became important as a seaport. Farmers shipped their grain down the great river systems that drained into the Mississippi. Ships from every country in the world tied up at the city docks, and the international flavor became even more pronounced.

Louis Armstrong's ancestors came to Louisiana as slaves, imported to work the great plantations. Louis himself felt that his ancestors came from the Gold Coast of Africa. There seemed to be none of the dilution of blood caused by intermarriage with lighter-skinned groups. Mayann came to New Orleans from Butte, Louisiana, to work as a servant girl to a white family, helping raise their children. She married Willie Armstrong when she was fifteen.

Like the other successive waves of immigrants, the black newcomers assimilated the Creole culture into their own African roots. Even the Christianized blacks retained much of the old religions, resulting in the voodoo cults and a superstitious outlook on life that lasts into this century.

In a 1966 interview with Richard Meryman for *Life* magazine, later expanded and published as a small book after his death, Louis remembered how as a small child he and the other children would crush bricks to make a bucket of red brick dust. They sold this dust to prostitutes on Saturday mornings, earning as much as fifty to seventy cents for their labor. When an adult laborer earned a dollar a day, this was good money for a youngster.

"Every Saturday," remembered Louis, "they'd scrub

their steps down with pee and then they'd throw the brick dust on the sidewalk in front of me and that brought them luck Saturday night.''

The girls of the district lived in cribs, rows of fifteen or twenty attached one-room structures under a single roof. Each room held a bed, a dresser, and a woman. There was no such thing as an indoor toilet, of course.

Elsewhere in the city, such a room might rent for eight dollars a month. The prostitutes paid $3.50 a day, which was collected by the agent for the landlord each evening before business began. A year's rental elsewhere for the entire row might total, $1,900; in the district, a small investment in land and building materials produced an income of $2,100 a month.

There was corruption, of course, at every level; the system could never have existed without it. Each week the police bagman came around to collect the pile of coins left on the steps by the girls, who might pay fifty cents or a dollar a day for their protection. The pile of coins might wait all day, but even the most foolhardy thief knew better than to succumb to the temptation.

This then was the world little Louis Armstrong knew as his playground and as his home. Perdido Street comes from a Spanish word meaning, literally, "the lost." In the early years of annual flooding the name was applied to many of the streets in the area, which became "lost" under the waters. In time, the name became fixed to the street that still carries it today. Yet during the early years of the twentieth century the name was particularly apt, for many of the souls who dwelt in Perdido Street were indeed lost to the salvation of heaven.

The people who lived back of the Quarter shared the superstitions of the prostitutes. Money in the best of times was scarce; there wasn't any way to spare for the doctor, so that worthy was never summoned for ordinary illnesses or simple wounds. Instead, Mayann and the other women of the district relied almost exclusively on home and folk remedies, some of which had come over from Africa.

When salve was needed to soothe cuts and wounds, several of the women would go to the railroad tracks and gather basketsful of pepper grass and other herbs. This was boiled until it was gummy. Since all of the children and many of the adults went barefoot even to school and to church, they were constantly picking up splinters and nails from the dirt-surfaced streets. The children played in the vacant lots, ran through buildings that were in such bad condition they had either collapsed or were being torn down. Sometimes they picked up broken pieces of glass. But the pepper grass salve worked every time.

One time Louis and several of his playmates were climbing over a pile of rubble where a house had been demolished, when a piece of slate fell off a roof next door and hit him on the head. He was knocked cold, and carried home by his frightened friends. Mayann and Mama Lucy boiled up the herbs and applied a poultice to the injury, then dosed Louis with Pluto water and put him to bed to sweat it out. The shock was so great that a form of lockjaw, possibly hysterical, set in.

The two women watched over Louis all night. When he woke in the morning he had a headache, but he was able to go to school as though nothing had happened.

Mayann also believed devoutly in the efficacy of a regular physic, to keep the system cleaned out. When Louis five or six, depending on the version accepted, Willie and Mayann again parted after one of their reconciliations. Mayann was sick in bed, unable to care for little Beatrice. She sent a neighbor woman to Josephine, to ask Willie's mother to let Louis come and help her out.

She half-expected her mother-in-law, to say no, but, as Louis recalled in *My Life in New Orleans,* Josephine dressed the boy in a new Buster Brown suit and sent him along with the neighbor woman. That day he had his first ride on a street car, and his first brush with Jim Crow.

"Since I was the first to get in," said Louis, almost fifty years later, "I walked right up to the front of the car without noticing the signs on the backs of the seats on both sides, which read FOR COLORED PASSENGERS ONLY. Thinking the woman was following me, I sat down in one of the front seats. However, she did not join me, and when I turned to see what had happened, there was no lady. Looking all the way to the back of the car, I saw her waving to me frantically.

" 'Come here, boy,' she cried. 'Sit where you belong.'

"I thought she was kidding me, so I stayed where I was, sort of acting cute. What did I care where she sat? Quick as a flash she dragged me to the back of the car and pushed me into one of the rear seats. Then I saw the signs."

Mayann, according to *My Life In New Orleans*, lived in a single room in a back courtyard, where she had to cook, wash, iron and take care of Mama Lucy. After greeting her son, her first act was to have him bring a box of Coal Roller Pills from her dresser drawer. These were very like Carter's Little Liver Pills, but if possible, even blacker.

She made Louis take three of the Coal Roller Pills right away, then sent him out to buy red beans and rice for their supper. The psychic worked as effectively as the pepper grass. From then on throughout his life, Louis continued to take a psychic regularly. In later years his favorite was a bedtime teaspoonful of an herbal mixture called Swiss Kriss. He was forever pressing it on his friends, many of whom accepted, to their regret. Whether or not he made any converts to his favorite remedy is unknown.

Reading Louis' two books, the reader does not get the feeling that he is actually listening to Louis Armstrong. He had a distinctive style of writing and of speaking that came over clearly to anyone who heard him, or received one of his many letters. Louis received a typewriter as a gift during the early 1930s, and was fond of using it.

His first book, *Swing That Music,* was published in 1936, but once the manuscript was in the hands of the publishers, something regrettable happened, it was almost completely rewritten. In the process, the publishers added material that hadn't been in the original, apparently in an effort to build up the reputation of the Original Dixieland Jazz Band as the seminal band in the genre. This, according to later writers, was a blatant lie, apparently pushed by the Original Dixieland Jazz Band's promoters.

Swing That Music is nonetheless an interesting book, for it was one of the first to attempt to describe the origins of jazz. It is also unique in that Louis, with Horace Gerlach, wrote a song of the same title, recording it for release at the same time as the book.

Ten famous jazz musicians of the day were then asked to score the song for their instruments, and the sheet music of those scores was published as fold-outs in the back of the book, for the reader to cut out. The ten musicians were an all-star cast of the middle 1930s, although at least half are probably remembered today only by jazz historians.

The rest became giants in the world of music. The ten were: clarinet, Benny Goodman; trombone, Tommy Dorsey; violin, Joe Venuti; trumpet, Louis himself; tenor sax, Bud Freeman; xylophone, Red Norvo; piano, Claude Hopkins; guitar, Carl Kress; bass, Stanley Dennis; and drums, Ray Bauduc.

I was fortunate enough to find an uncut copy of what is now a very rare volume in a university library. The book is well worth the search, for the scores alone. *My Life In New Orleans* fared no better in the hands of its publisher, although this time the spirit of Louis' words was honored. It is said the French edition is most faithful to the original, for it was translated directly from the manuscript and not from the published book.

3
GROWING UP IN
NEW ORLEANS

3

Growing Up In New Orleans

Mayann had other Creole remedies in her stock of medicines. For sore throats, she gathered cockroaches and boiled them, straining off the water and giving the liquid a teaspoonful at a time. To cut a cold she prescribed Sweet Spirits of Nitre, with a little sugar, in hot water. This became another remedy that Louis was to use throughout his life, although in different fashion. He put it on his face and his lips when they cracked from blowing the horn. The pain of the Spirits hitting an open crack was almost beyond belief, but Louis said the misery passed quickly. Again, it worked.

To the end of his life, Louis kept a book of Creole remedies and sayings, *Gumbo Ya-Ya*. It was many years before he switched his faith from the folk medicine of his childhood to conventional doctoring.

When Louis returned from that first errand for his mother, he found the one-room house filled with a crowd, all of whom turned out to be his cousins. He had never before met any of them, but they were the children of Uncle Ike Miles. Ike Miles apparently was Mayann's uncle. There were Isaac and Aaron, Jerry and Willie, Louisa and Sarah Ann, and baby Flora.

Ike Miles was a widower. To support his brood, he worked on the levees, unloading cargo boats. The money was irregular, but somehow the family managed to survive. The whole lot lived in one room, as many crowded into the one bed as it would hold. The rest slept on the floor.

Whenever Mayann's eyes began to roam and she got the urge to go out on the town, she dumped Louis and Mama Lucy on Uncle Ike. This happened often enough that the Miles' house became a second home for the children. In later life, Louis remembered his cousins as being so lazy that they broke the china so they wouldn't have to wash the dishes. Consequently, everyone ate from tin plates.

Red beans and rice were the staples of the diet for the blacks of New Orleans, and popular with the whites and the Creoles as well. Sometimes a chunk of meat, salt pork, was tossed into the pot for flavoring. For the rest of Louis' life it remained his favorite dish.

After the boy moved back permanently with his mother, he grew used to the "stepfathers" that were in constant attendance on Mayann. Over the years, Louis remembered later, there were a dozen or more. Mayann was a stout women, fond of her own cooking; by then she usually worked as a cook for white families. But she was still good-looking, and respected by everyone who knew her. Jovial and convivial, she never had any trouble attracting male companionship.

The nicest of all of Louis' stepfathers was a man named Gabe. He was neither very smart nor well-educated, but Gabe was blessed with the common sense that seemed lacking in most of Mayann's liaisons. Gabe worked on the coal wagons, where Louis spent much of his time over a period of several years. Slim was another stepfather who could be nice when he was sober, but he drank far too much. Albert was the worst; he liked to beat on little Louis.

One day Albert and Mayann were sitting on the canal bank while Louis played nearby. They quarreled, and suddenly Albert became enraged and began to curse Mayann. Then he struck her in the face, knocking her into the water, and walked off without a single backward glance.

Louis began to yell for help while Mayann, her face bloody from the blow, screamed in the water. Bystanders came running and managed to rescue her, but Louis remained frightened for a long time afterward.

That was the last the Armstrongs saw of Albert, which probably was fortunate for him. Louis had vowed to kill him, should their paths cross again. Vengeance was a sudden and direct thing in those days of violence. In later years his hatred remained strong, but at last he heard that Albert had died of other causes.

Despite the grinding poverty in which the Armstrongs and most of the blacks of the district lived, Louis remembered his childhood as a happy time. In those days in New Orleans music seemed to fill the air everywhere. He heard it in church, in school, even in the streets.

Funky Butt Hall was on Perdido Street. In *Horn of Plenty,* another rare Armstrong biography by Belgian author Robert Goffin and first published in America in 1947, the name of the dance hall was described in unrestrained prose as: ". . . that ill-smelling establishment. Its very name graphically characterizing the awful smell that always pervaded the air after the dances were over. They were totally unrestrained in their lewdness, and the black dancers' sweaty bodies heightened the general atmosphere of depravity. So much for 'Funky.' As for 'Butt,' the word is the diminutive applied to the posteriors that shook so vigorously during the gyrations of the dance . . .''

Goffin's descriptions should be taken with a grain of salt. I have been unable to findy any corroborating evidence that this was indeed the derivation of the name; yet it could be the truth. On the other hand, in *Slang and Its Analogues,* a dictionary of slang published in seven volumes between 1890 and 1904, "funky" is explained as an adjective meaning nervous, frightened, timid. At this point in time the true meaning of the name will probably never be known. It could as easily have been named after its proprietor, considering the fondness of the blacks of the time for nicknames. (Max Jones says that it was the Masonic Hall, nicknamed the Funky Butt.)

Dances were held in the hall every Saturday night. The band played out front for perhaps half an hour to draw business, while the kids of the neighborhood gathered to try the dances the adults would do inside. When the band retired into the building, the children glued their eyes to the cracks in the wall.

The hall was just a large room with a bandstand, but it was popular in the district; and the dancing (as in Goffin's description) sometimes became wild. Louis remembered the young girls shaking everything they had, slapping themselves on the backside while the band belted out such favorites as *The Bucket's Got a Hole In It.*

At the end of the night, if no major fights had broken out, the dancers performed a quadrille as the last number of the evening. Everyone lined up, then crossed over in figured movements that Louis remembered being beautiful.

Fights, however, were common. The men carried their razors even on the dance floor. If a man wanted to show particular respect for his girl, something that didn't happen very often, he crooked his left elbow out and rested his hat on it. The hat was usually a fancy Stetson, for which the men saved their money for months to buy. The dance was allowed to finish before any action was taken. If the hat had been touched by another dancer, as soon as the band stopped playing the hat's owner sought out the offender and belted him in the mouth.

Almost as common as fights, and loved by everyone, young and old, were the parades. The social clubs of the district in particular took pride in dressing up and showing off their finery and their bands. They played the music that was then called ragtime, had earlier been called levee camp music. Later it became known as jazz, originally spelled "jass." No one has ever adequately defined the meaning of jazz, or explained the derivation of the term. Goffin ascribes a sexual meaning to the original spelling, a theory ascribed to by other authoritis; but it is only a theory.

The social clubs would parade at any excuse, but funeral parades were most common of all. The clubs held wakes for their members who had passed on; some joined more than one club to insure a larger turn-out of mourners. Sometimes the singing became so loud the body in the coffin rocked right along with the singers. Sometimes, before embalming became standard practice, and medicine itself was still uncertain, the body sat up right in the middle of the wake.

"Goddamn," Louis said later to Richard Meryman, "imagine all them people trying all at once to get out of one little bitty door."

During the funeral the musicians waited outside the church for the services to finish. The Catholics were popular because they had short funerals, but sometimes it seemed as though the Baptists would stay in the church until eternity itself arrived. However, there was always a barroom on the corner to make the waiting easier.

When the coffin was finally brought out, the band walked along with it, slowly and with many halts, playing funeral marches. The drummers put a handerchief under the snare to soften the sound and give it a tom-tom effect.

Once the body was in the grave and the last words had been said, the drummer tightened his snares again and hit a long roll. Then the band marched back to the social club, playing music that celebrated the joy of the moment, now that the deceased had presumably been welcomed into heaven. The most popular songs for the march back were *When the Saints Go Marching In* and *Didn't He Ramble.*

The funeral parade was always followed by a "second line"—spectators gathered for no other reason than to enjoy the music. There were many children and adults in raggedy pants and without coats, sometimes with one suspender hanging down. On the way home the paraders stopped frequently for a brief taste in a bar, for it was a well-known fact that blowing a horn dries the throat and creates a terrible thirst.

During those pauses the second line held the horses and the instruments, and when the band members came out again, they gave a drink to those who performed such services. As Louis grew a little bigger, he frequently held Joe Oliver's trumpet, a valuable service that paid off handsomely in the long run. Then back at the social club, there'd be another keg of beer, and a celebration to rejoice.

Once each year the social clubs of the district joined together for the biggest parade of all. Everyone wore silk shirts, white hats and black pants, and had streamers across their chests with the name of their club emblazoned in gold or silver letters. Those who could were on horseback, and there were frequent stops along the line of march at houses of club members, where as usual a fresh keg of beer waited the thirsty revelers. Frequently the parade finished at the fairgrounds, with a giant picnic.

The social clubs had colorful names: the Broadway Swells, the Bulls, the Turtles, the Moneywasters. The latter used to carry a big cabbage with cigars and paper dollars sticking out of it. Louis later joined the Tammany Social Club.

Parades and funerals weren't the only occasion for celebration and for band music. On Saturdays, furniture wagons were turned into portable bandstands, usually with signs on their sides advertising dance halls or prize fights. The musicians wore their uniforms—all of the best bands were uniformed, usually with a music lyre on the military collar and the name of the band on the caps. The wagons stopped at street corners to play awhile, attracting an audience; then they moved on.

The music was lively, the audience enthralled. Best of all, however, was when two bands arrived at the same corner at the same time. The wagons pulled up alongside each other and the bands held impromptu "cutting" contests to see which was best in the eyes of the people gathered around. Sometimes the hustlers and pimps of that block chained the wagon wheels together, forcing the bands to stay at the corner while they blew themselves into exhaustion.

It was in those bands, whether in the parades or on the advertising wagons and in dance halls such as the Funky Butt, that Louis Armstrong first heard the music that was rapidly developing into jazz. It was also played in the honky tonks and in the sporting houses, but there were few if any opportunities for a little boy to hear the latter.

Joe Oliver was Louis' favorite almost from the beginning; he earned the title "King" after Buddy Bolden's unhappy removal to the sanitarium. Other played with the Onward Brass Band, and Louis used to follow him around. Unlike most of the musicians, Joe Oliver did not drink; but he went into the bars to talk with the men. Later, when Louis was first getting started, Oliver gave him one of his old horns, the first good instrument Louis ever had.

The Onward Brass Band was one of the most famous, but there were many others, including the Crescent City Band and Robichaud's. Music was in the very streets, filled the very air. Peddlers such as the pie man and the waffle man made music to draw their customers—the pie man had a bugle and the waffle man a large triangle. Lonzo the junk man had a long tin horn, such as children play on Christmas and on New Year's Eve. He could play his tin horn like a trumpet, even belt out the blues.

Like most of his playmates and from necessity, Louis hustled after pennies and nickles, running errands and selling newspapers. The brick dust scheme mentioned earlier was just one of many ways of making the money that Mayann could not give him out of her pocket. For a time Louis worked with Lonzo, buying old clothes in rich neighborhoods. While Lonzo played his tin horn, it was Louis' job to yell out, "Old rags and bones, lady! Old rags and bones!"

Later, (much later, according to *My Life in New Orleans*), he worked on Morris Karnofsky's coal wagon, yelling: "Stone coal, lady! Nickel a water bucket! Stone coal, nickel a water bucket!" Stone coal was anthracite, hard coal.

In the interview with Richard Meryman, Louis remembered: "The bottoms of those buckets was all pounded up so maybe three or four big lumps would fill it. We was selling all through the red-light district—it was called Storyville. The women would be standing there in the doorways to their cribs, wearing their "teddies"—that was a famous uniform they had, all silk, like baby bloomers only transparent. One of them would call, 'Commere boy. Bring me three buckets.' And it was fun for me to go in them cribs and for a quarter extra start them fires. And I'd take my little quick peek, you know, scared she'd catch me, slap me and shove me out of there. But they didn't pay me no mind. Just a stone-coal boy, breathin' like a bitch."

Most of the whores who worked in Storyville were white or light Creoles or mulattoes. The only black musician who played in the famous houses was Jelly Roll Morton, the piano player. While in Storyville he got the gold tooth with a diamond in it, for which he later became famous.

The most famous of Storyville's many famous madames was Lulu White and her Mahagony Hall. Lulu was a black woman, but according to Louis, she had no blacks working for her, not even maids. The rich men came from miles around to visit Lulu's sporting house.

Storyville itself covered thirty-eight blocks, centered around Basin Street. The prostitutes came from all over the country, by boat and by train, flooding in to take advantage of the legally sanctioned industry. The street girls were forced out by the establishment of the district, unable to afford the rents. Many were homeless, wandered the streets with a carpet rolled over their shoulder; they couldn't even afford a crib in a row house. They took their customers wherever there was room to spread their rug, charging as little as twenty-five cents.

Those businessmen and businesswomen who owned sporting houses in other parts of the city objected strenuously to the new district. But even the Supreme Court of Louisiana upheld New Orleans' method of dealing with the problem. Unbroken lines of cafes, saloons, gambling halls and flophouses stretched for blocks along the streets of Storyville. And there were the houses themselves. The motto of Storyville was "Anything you like, Mister, any way you want it."

Drugs were no real problem in those days, for most drugs could be had without prescription from your friendly neighborhood pharmacist. In 1907, cocaine sold for a dime a gram. The first Federal regulations took effect in 1908, shooting the price to half a dollar. Later, it went up to a dollar or two. Marijuana was undoubtedly available, for possession was not changed from a misdemeanor to a felony until 1937. More about that later.

Few people today realize that Coca Cola was given its

name because the original formula included cocaine. Many other soft drinks of the time included habit-forming drugs, as did most of the patent medicines. The establishment of the Pure Food and Drug Administration did a great deal to save the lives of scores of millions of Americans, but there are many today who would like to see at least a few of the regulations relaxed in a return to the good old days before 1907.

In some of the fancier sporting houses of Storyville, a customer not in formal evening attire felt out of place. The next morning he arose to find his shirt freshly laundered and his suit pressed. The houses were among the first buildings in the city to install electric lighting, stained glass windows and heavy decorations in the most elegant manner of the Gay 90s, which meant heavy velvets, scattered ottomans and love seats, cozy private alcoves with embroidered pillows, and heavy framed pictures of the President of the United States and William Shakespeare.

Some of the houses issued coupon books: buy now, use a ticket each time you visited. Others sent notices of special attractions to favored clients. Thousands of people were employed in the district. After dark, there was noise and excitement, music and action, all night long.

The only way Louis Armstrong could have seen Storyville was on the coal cart. A policeman called the Corporal patrolled the district, carrying a big stick. He was notorious for breaking legs.

Gravier Street was where the black girls sat on their doorsteps, front doors open, calling to passersby, "Hello, Daddy, want to do a little business?"

Storyville finally came to the end of its days of glory in 1917. The United States had entered World War I, and both the army and the navy protested loudly over the diseases picked up in the district by their recruits. The services demanded that Storyville be shut down, or the whole city would be placed out of bounds.

City officials took their protests to Washington, D.C., but to no avail. New Orleans was forced to pass an ordinance that as of midnight, November 12, prostitution would be illegal everywhere in the city. Despite the protests of girls and customers alike, the end came quietly; and with it ended Louis' chance to play in the famous saloons and honky-tonks of the district.

But that was yet to come. As a small boy, Louis bought his newspapers from a white boy, who later became one of his closest friends. When he was eleven or twelve, he formed a singing quartet with his playmates, Little Mack, Big Nose Sidney and Georgie Grey. An occasional member of the group was Red Head Happy, but he used to come in just long enough to grab the money. A bully, he finally quit to become a pimp. Later, he became famous as a drummer.

The boys put on long pants and went all over the district, singing for the girls and their pimps. Louis sang tenor and played a slide whistle for accompaniment. Their theme song was *My Brazilian Beauty*.

My Brazilian beauty down on the Amazon,
That's where my baby's gone, gone, gone!

Louis frequently dreamed of the Brazilian beauty on the Amazon, but in those days he didn't even know there was such a country as Brazil. Later, when he visited South America on tour, the words to the old song came back to him.

Passing the hat brought the quartet as much as seventy-five cents or a dollar each. At that time Mayann washed clothes for a white family on Canal Street, boiling them in a big tin tub over a little coal furnace in the back yard of her employer's house. She earned a dollar a day.

It was along about then that Mayann first got religion. Elder Cozy's church was directly across the street from the house where she lived with her children, and the elder was one of the most popular preachers in all of New Orleans. When the preacher hit his stride, the whole church rocked along with him.

Louis was forced to attend the services with his mother, although it's questionable whether or not he shared Mayann's fervor. She became so excited listening to the elder's stirring words that one time she began to sway from side to side along with the preacher, at last knocking Louis right off the bench. It took six strong brothers to calm her down, while Louis broke up in laughter.

He paid for it later, of course, When they got home Mayann lit into Louis with her switch. Later, she was baptized in the Mississippi, ducked so many times into the water that Louis thought she was drowning.

Louis was usually Dipper to his friends. All his life he was bad on names. so he usually made up nicknames on the spot. Later, his friends became used to calling him "Gate," and later yet, "Pops." The latter became as much his nickname as was Satchmo.

The people of New Orleans seized on any excuse for a celebration: funerals, parades, birthdays, holidays. But the biggest single night of the year was New Year's Eve. Everyone in the district brought out their firecrackers and roman candles, their pistols and anything else that would make a loud and satisfying noise.

On New Year's Eve, December 31st, 1912, Louis and

the quartet were swinging along Rampart Street, singing *My Brazilian Beauty*. In Louis' pocket was a .38 pistol that belonged to his current stepfather. He had discovered it a week earlier, hidden in Mayann's trunk. All week, whenever the opportunity arose, he had dug it out.

Like any young boy, the gun held a near-fatal attraction for Louis. Add New Year's Eve, and the temptation became overwhelming. This night the pistol was loaded with blanks; Louis strutted along with chest out, feeling as though he were cock of the walk and king of the world.

Suddenly a boy on the other side of the street pulled out a gun, probably a cap pistol, and emptied it at the quartet. The challenge could not be allowed to pass. At the urging of his friends, Louis returned the fire, emptying the 38. into the air.

The effect was grand; the .38 made a great deal of noise. Frightened, the other boy took off like a scared rabbit, vanquished from the field of battle.

The quartet resumed their march down the street, laughing and shouting. Louis reloaded the .38 with blanks and from sheer exuberance emptied it again. But this time, as the last shot echoed down Rampart Street, a pair of strong arms suddenly caught him from behind.

At first the boy thought his heart had stopped. It was a cold night, but sweat poured down Louis' face. The man held him tight while he squirmed frantically, watching the other members of the quartet scatter to the winds. Soon he was alone with his captor.

Louis had been captured by a police detective, a white man. The boy begged to be allowed to return to his mother; the .38 had been confiscated. The detective listened without emotion, refusing to relent. Louis' luck had run out.

The policeman took the boy to juvenile court, where the judge ordered him locked up for the night. It was an unhappy ending to what had been started as a joyous occasion. Scared almost sick, Louis spent the night on a hard cot in a cell. This was his first serious run-in with the law, and already he was in jail!

Louis woke early; the time passed slowly until the turnkey finally opened the door at ten o'clock and told him to come out. The man eyed him carefully.

"Louis Armstrong?"

"Yessir."

"You're goin' to the Colored Waifs' Home for Boys."

(Again, the actual sequence of events is clouded. One source says Louis was sent to the Home, then returned two weeks later for a hearing before the juvenile court. Another says that he was sent at least twice to the Home, returned once to his mother and then sent back. Louis himself, in a letter to Max Jones, could not remember two separate commitments; nor were there any mention of two separate events in either of his two books.)

The fact that Louis had never been in trouble before meant nothing. He was a street urchin, and the detective had said that he had violated the law. Perhaps a white boy from a similar poverty-stricken background would have received the same summary judgment, and perhaps not. Louis was black.

He was taken into the yard of the jail, where a Black Maria waited with two strong horses between the traces, and shoved inside. There were several other boys in the wagon, arrested for similar offenses. The door slammed shut and the horses started out, jerking the wagon into motion.

The door of the Black Maria had a tiny grilled window that showed a little square of sky and an equally tiny part of the buildings they passed in the streets. Frightened as he was, Louis was miserable during his ride to the Waifs' Home. Despite its name, the Colored Waifs' Home for Boys was a reform school, with wooden bars on the windows of the dormitories to discourage escapes.

Louis Armstrong had no way of knowing in that dark moment, nor in the dark weeks to come, that his life had just been drastically changed. . . for the better.

During the next year and a half, while in the custody of the Waifs' Home, he was taught to play the cornet.

4
THE HOME

4

The Home

The Colored Waifs' Home for Boys was located in the countryside, outside the city limits of New Orleans. A streetcar line came within a few blocks, and once Louis was established in the Home, Mayann and Mama Lucy visited him regularly.

The Home was an old building that had originally been used for other purposes, in an almost idyllic pastoral setting. Across the road was a large diary farm, the fields and meadows filled with what Louis later remembered as hundreds of browsing cattle. This in itself must have been an unusual sight to the boys who arrived with Louis, for it's doubtful that any of them had been further from back of the Quarter than Rampart Street or Canal Street.

(Once, after school let out for the day, Louis hurried

to the house where Mayann was then working. The white family that employed her were away for the day. She gave him a guided tour of the house, and he afterward recalled the marvels of the tiled bathroom and the kitchen, and furnishings that were beyond his wildest dreams.)

It's possible that a few of the families around Perdido and Gravier Streets kept a few chickens or other livestock, but there was nothing like the cows and horses that freely roamed the fields across from the Home. There were calves with the cows, and even a few bulls. The sight was memorable enough to stay with Louis the rest of his life.

The lawns surrounding the Colored Waifs' Home were shaded with a number of old trees. As Louis later remembered the morning, when he stepped out of the Black Maria for the first time his nostrils filled with the scent of flowers he did not recognize. He asked someone what they were, and was told honeysuckle.

Here again, it seems likely that Louis' memory failed him; either that, or he arrived at the Home on two separate occasions. Honeysuckle is a summer flower; it could not have been in bloom on the first day of the New Year. Undoubtedly the Home was flooded with the scent of honeysuckle in the summertime, but certainly not then. It is more likely that magnolia were in bloom, but these should have been familiar to him from the city. Whatever the truth of Louis' first arrival at Home, honeysuckle remained a favorite flower throughout the rest of his life.

Captain Joseph Jones and his wife ran the Home, aided by Mr. Alexander and Mr. Peter Davis. They were called wadens, or keepers; the boys were called inmates. The boys were in the midst of lunch when the new arrivals entered the building for the first time and were ushered down a long corridor to the mess hall.

The boys sat at long tables, eating a simple meal of white beans without rice. The food served at the Home was always plain, although plentiful; the boys did much of the cooking themselves, as part of their regular chores.

Louis should have been hungry, for he had not eaten since supper the previous night. He was given a seat at the end of a table and a plate of beans was passed down to him. But frightened and worried, he had no appetite for food. Unable to make himself eat, he stared at the plate for awhile, at last pushed it away.

His appetite did not return for several days. The shock of being thrown into a new environment was more than Louis could accept. The keepers observed his behavior without comment, did nothing to encourage him to eat. On the fourth day he woke up so hungry that he was first in the breakfast line.

The adults broke out in laughter when they saw him. This would indicate a less than sympathetic attitude, perhaps a certain callousness to the plight of a boy who had been ripped from the only life he knew and plunged into an entirely new environment, to sink or to survive on his own.

There were boys as young as eight or nine in the Home, and as old as eighteen. Some came from the surrounding small towns, so the Home was not strictly a New Orleans operation. The keepers were all black, as were Miss Spriggins, who taught the lower grades, and Mrs. Vignes, who taught the upper.

Captain Jones had military experience, having served in the cavalry. Every morning he drilled the boys in the Manual of Arms, in the court in front of the building.

For guns, they were given wooden rifles.

Just how much education, apart from music, Louis or any of the boys received at the Home is a matter of conjecture. Louis said later that his formal education stopped with the fifth grade. While living with his mother, he attended the Fisk School, although like so much of his early life, the records of his attendance have been lost.

As he was twelve (or thirteen, as one source insists) at the time of his commitment to the Waifs' Home, that would indicate that he was in the fifth grade at the time of his arrest. The authority in charge of the Home encouraged the boys to learn a vocation. They were given their choice, if one of the limited number of subjects available proved of more interest than another.

Mr. Alexander taught carpentry, gardening, and how to build campfires. The first two were certainly useful crafts, but what use the boys could make of the latter in earning a living has not been explained, unless they intended to become scoutmasters.

Peter Davis was bandmaster, and taught music.

Davis was to prove the most important influence of Louis Armstrong's life. Yet at the time Louis first arrived at the Home, Davis showed him nothing but animosity. The bandmaster knew that he came from The Battlefield, the worst section of the worst district in all of New Orleans. Even the Fisk School had a reputation for having the worst pupils in the city. He assumed that any boy in trouble from the district must be either a serious offender, or incorrigible.

Some of the boys were repeaters, committed time after time to the Home; during Louis' stay, at least one was there for the fourth time. Ocasionally a new boy came in filthy and covered with lice. When that happened the newcomer's head was shaved and his clothes were thrown into the fire kept burning under the big laundry kettle in the back yard.

All of the chores of the Home were done by the boys, including the laundry and mending of their own clothing. The building was kept spotlessly clean, for there was never a shortage of labor to scrub the floors, wash and iron, or work in the yard or the kitchen. Once a boy adjusted to the fact that he was there to stay, until released by the judge who had committed him, most got along well enough.

The boys were not mistreated, although punishment could be swift and harsh. One day Louis broke some unimportant rule, which normally would have brought only a scolding. Unfortunately, the infraction was observed by Peter Davis. The bandmaster gave him fifteen hard whacks on the hand.

Freedom remained a sweet lure to many of the boys. Despite the wooden bars on the windows, it was not difficult for a determined boy to escape. One night a boy tied half a dozen sheets together and greased his body to help him slip through the bars.

He made his escape, although the other boys were afraid they'd be blamed for helping him. To their surprise, the keepers accepted the escape with equanimity.

"He'll be back," they said.

They were right. Less than a week later the runaway was returned by the police: exhausted, dirty from sleeping under old houses or in whatever shelter he could find, and hungry as well.

The adults said nothing to the boy during the rest of the day; Louis and the others thought he was going to be let off the hook, his misadventures during his freedom considered suffering and punishment enough. They were mistaken.

At bedtime that night the boys were told to dress in their pajamas and gather around; the runaway was kept naked after he undressed. The four strongest boys in the Home held his arms and legs while Captain Jones gave him a hundred and five lashes.

. The audience yelled as loudly as the punished boy, but to no avail. Any thoughts Louis and some of the others may have harbored of escape evaporated with that object lesson. However, others were to try it later, always to be caught and returned. During Louis' term in the Home, not a single runaway remained free.

The older boys were punished the most harshly. Once, while the boys were on a work party about a mile from the Home, cutting trees, an eighteen year-old boy called Houma—after his small home town—took off suddenly. Mr. Alexander sent Willie Davis, a boy of the same age and the fastest runner in the Home, after him. Willie caught Houma and told him he had to go back.

That night Houma received a brutal punishment: five hundred lashes.

Life for the boys was regulated by the bugle. They woke up in the morning to reveille, assembled for the march to mess call, and went to bed to the clear notes of reveille. From the start, Louis envied the buglar more than any of the other boys, because he had the opportunity to play his instrument so often. The work parties might take them a mile or more away, but the call of the bugle carried everywhere, the boys dropping what they were doing to hotfoot it back to the mess hall.

After Louis' first few days of rough adjustment to his fate, his interest turned to the regular band rehearsals. Peter Davis rebuffed his overtures of interest. The bandmaster made no attempt to hide his dislike for Louis.

Louis was a happy-to-lucky youngster, liked by everyone. He couldn't understand why Peter Davis hated him. Even when Davis finally relented and let Louis join the band, it was some time before the boy came to trust the man who held the key to his future.

After Davis' dislike became clear, Louis tried to avoid the bandmaster. When the band gathered for rehearsal, however, he crept as close as he could, frequently hiding in a corner. Davis was a good teacher, and Louis enjoyed listening to the other boys practice.

Peter Davis was able to inspire the youngsters in his band to play their instruments to the very best of their ability. The program was varied, included a little of almost every kind of music—except ragtime. Davis abhorred the raucous noise of the latter.

From the first, Louis was most intrigued by the cornet, perhaps inspired by his memories of Buddy Bolden, Joe Oliver and Bunk Johnson. He had already decided that the cornet was the only instrument for him. He didn't switch to the trumpet until a dozen years later; the smaller cornet was preferred by almost all New Orleans musicians.

Louis wanted desperately to be a part of the band, but he dared not ask Peter Davis to let him join. He had no idea how long he would be kept in the Home, because Judge Wilson had given him an indeterminate sentence. That meant that only Judge Wilson could release him, and that would not happen unless an important white person vouched for both Louis and for Mayann and Willie Armstrong as well.

Louis natural musical talent came to the attention of Peter Davis in a roundabout fashion. He was first given the chance to sing by Miss Spriggins and then by Mrs. Vignes, when he was promoted to her class. By then several months had passed, and he had reconciled himself to a long stay in the Home.

Little by little, listening to Louis' clear tenor, Davis began to unfreeze. Sometimes the bandmaster even offered him a smile of approval. Louis did whatever chores were assigned to him and rarely fractured even the small rules.

He didn't need much encouragement, once he realized that Davis wasn't going to hit him for the most trifling reason. He stopped hiding while listening to rehearsals, and soon assumed his former happy frame of mind even around the bandmaster. Peter Davis tolerated his presence.

Perhaps six months passed; by then, Louis had completely adapted to the Home. At supper one night, a plain meal of black strap molasses and bread that by then seemed as satisfying as a homecooked chicken dinner, the bandmaster stopped by Louis' table just as the boys started to get up.

"Louis, how would you like to join our brass band?"

Louis was speechless. He stared at the bandmaster while Davis repeated the question, at last managed to stammer a reply. Davis patted him on the back and told him to wash up, and come to the evening rehearsal.

While washing, Louis' thoughts were entirely on his good fortune: at last he'd have a chance to play the cornet! Wouldn't that make the gang in his old neighborhood sit up and take a second look!

He fantasized himself playing with the masters: Joe Oliver and Bunk Johnson. In the excitement, he got soap in his eyes. He rushed to the rehearsal hall. . .

His dreams crumbled as the bandmaster handed him

a tambourine.

Louis remembered later that he was deeply disappointed by the humble instrument; but he managed to hide his feelings and took his place with the band. When the music began he shook the tambourine in close rhythm. The beat of the music seemed to be part of him, seemed to be in his bloodstream as the instruments played. Louis had been born to play music, and to sing.

Peter Davis was pleased with his discovery. After the number finished, he switched Louis to the drums, because the boy had the beat for which he had been searching. Almost fifty years later, Louis recalled that the song was *After the Animal's Ball*, a popular hit of the day. There was a break in the middle for a drum roll, and Louis hit it with everything he had.

The boys loved what Louis did, and even the bandmaster showed his approval. Davis needed an alto horn player even more than he did a drummer; he gave Louis the horn. The alto usually replaces the french horn in a brass band.

It must have taken Louis some time to learn the new instrument, for his only previous experience with horns was the slide whistle he had played with the singing quartet. Yet his musical talent helped him, and soon enough he was proficient on the alto.

When evening rehearsals finished, the band drilled the other boys to bed. Dawdling was never tolerated. The keepers dispensed quick justice when they caught a slacker, and their years of experience had taught Captain Jones and the others just how long it took a boy to dress or undress and do whatever else was necessary.

Almost from the day he arrived at the Home, Louis had been popular with the other boys. Now he became as well-liked by the staff. One happy day the bugler was released to his parents. Peter Davis promptly gave the bugle to Louis.

He was coming closer to his dream. The bugle was battered, and none of his predecessors had even bothered to give it a cleaning. For that matter, most of the instruments were old, cast-offs from unknown former owners. The Home had no budget to cover such items. Peter Davis depended on outside contributions. Perhaps that was why the band accepted every possible outside engagement, performing in parades and at private picnics and other such social affairs.

Louis set out to clean the bugle. By the time he finished buffing the brass, the instrument positively gleamed. And when he played the horn the tones he produced seemed mellow and pure, unlike what the other boys had been able to force from the bell.

Satisfied with Louis' progress at whatever he was given, the bandmaster at last gave him his first cornet and taught him to play *Home Sweet Home.* Louis was in seventh heaven. From that time he practiced faithfully every day, quickly picking up the fingering and different tonalities of the instrument. At last, Peter Davis made Louis leader of the band.

This was an important step up, although Louis had already become a key man in the Home's orchestra. Until then, he had played at rehearsals, but apparently not for the outside engagements. Now he traveled with the other boys, even to the popular summer resort towns at West End and Spanish Town, and Milenburg and Little Woods.

The band members had their own uniforms for these forays into the outside world: long white pants turned up to resemble knickers, black sneakers, black stockings, thin blue garbardine jackets, and caps with black and white head bands. As leader, Louis wore a contrasting uniform: cream-colored pants, brown sneakers and stockings, and a cream-colored cap.

Sometimes the parades lasted for many hours, could go on all day, until even the most famous brass bands complained of aching feet and sore lips from blowing their instruments. The boys from the Home never griped, no matter how arduous the performance. One day they were hired by the Merry-Go-Round Social Club for a parade that ended up at Carrolton, a distance of almost twenty-five miles. The boys played every step of the way, and loved every minute of the day.

Word soon got back to Louis' old neighborhood that Dipper had become an important member of the band; and then Davis accepted an engagement for a prade that brought the band to Perdido Street. All of the whores and their pimps, the gamblers, the thieves and the beggars, turned out to see Mayann's boy marching in the parade.

As yet, they did not know that Louis had been promoted. Even Mayann hadn't been told. She was working a night job at the time, and sound asleep when the parade swung into the neighborhood. Dipper was spotted, swinging along out front, and somebody ran to wake his mother.

Flustered, Mayann came running to see her son strutting along as proud as a peacock. At that moment, Louis felt as though his heart would burst would pride. The neighborhood gang cheered him on, and someone asked Peter Davis if they could give Louis some money.

The bandmaster gave his permission, thinking any collection in this district wouldn't amount to very much. The hat was passed—Louis' hat. By the time the collection ended, he had to borrow hats from several of the other boys, to hold all of the money.

Peter Davis was flabbergasted. There was enough money to buy new uniforms and new instruments for the entire band. The band returned to the Home in triumph, and to show the gratitude of the staff for the generosity of Louis' friends, Davis talked Captain and Mrs. Jones into giving Louis permission to visit the city, and his mother, by himself.

Even while at the Home, Louis was touched by the music of the famous bands of New Orleans. Lying in his bunk on a quiet Sunday night, he could hear half a mile away Freddie Keppard and his band, playing for rich white folks. The sweet music on the evening air and the sweet scent of the honeysuckle were memories never forgotten.

Keppard was a good cornet man, with a style of his own, beautiful tone, and a marvelous endurance. Keppard was always one of Louis' favorites, although in his opinion, Bunk Johnson had the best one of all. Whenever Keppard played in a street parade he put a handkerchief over his hands, so no other cornet player could see his fingering. This Louis laughed at, in later days. Any good cornet player could have copied Keppard's style just by listening.

The eighteen months Louis spent in the Waifs' Home were a time of growing up. Looking back in later life, he felt that in that year and a half he had become a man. He had achieved respect from the other boys, from his family and friends, and at last from the staff.

Now that period in Louis' life was about to come to an end. It would be some time before the good times returned.

5
GETTING STARTED

5

Getting Started

After eighteen months, Willie Armstrong managed to have his son released from the Waifs' Home. Willie's employer at the turpentine factory put in a good word for Willie, and Judge Wilson made it a condition of Louis' parole that he live with is father and stepmother, Gertrude. Willie had remarried, happily, and now had two sons, Willie and Henry. The Armstrongs lived at Miro and Poydras Streets in the heart of The Battlefield.

Louis wasn't at all sure that he wanted to leave the Home. He had never lived with his father, and he didn't even know his stepmother and half brothers. Mayann and Mama Lucy visited him at the Home at every opportunity, but Willie hadn't come once.

His last evening at the Home was a warm night in

June; the air was heavy with the scent of honeysuckle. While Louis packed his few belongings, the band played a farewell concert. He joined them for several numbers, the first time Willie Armstrong had ever heard his son play. Willie was pleased and told Louis he must keep up with his music.

Mrs. Jones kissed him good-bye, and he shook hands with Captain Jones, Mr. Alexander and Peter Davis. Then he did the same with every boy there.

Louis' heart was heavy as he followed his father to the corner where they could catch the street car. He considered asking Willie to take him back and let him stay in the Home. But the moment passed, and when he reached his new home, he was welcomed by Gertrude Armstrong.

Gertrude was a loving woman, with more than enough affection to share with her husband, her own two sons, and her stepson. Louis soon learned to love her as well and to love his youngest half brother, Henry. Little Willie was another matter. The boy was constantly into mischief, his greatest delight seeming to come from upsetting the applecart for others. It seemed as though he had all the orneriness of the devil himself in his blood.

Since both Willie and Gertrude worked, Louis was left to take care of his half brothers. His parents soon found that he could cook and had a special way with beans. He took care of the household chores, but most of his time was given over to watching his brothers. Little Willie seemed to have a hollow leg; the food would disappear from the lunch table before Louis had a chance to sit down himself. He learned to eat before he called his brothers to the meal, in self-protection.

Just how long Louis stayed with Willie and Gertrude

is uncertain. Max Jones says that he didn't touch a horn for eighteen months to two years, but Louis himself, in *My Life in New Orleans,* said he practiced almost every day. At first his brothers laughed, but they soon learned better. They became entranced with the sounds he could produce.

In the interview with Richard Meryman, Louis said: "I started playing right away. Any time a cat would lay off, they'd say, 'Run get little Louis'—I was a little bitty fellow—and I got to play with them good musicians. But I couldn't get enough money together to even talk about a horn of my own—used to rent one for each gig. Then I found a little nickel-plate cornet for $10 in Uncle Jake's pawn shop—all bent up, holes knocked in the bell. It was a Tonk Brothers—ain't never heard of them. Charlie—he was the ofay fellow supplied me with papers when I was a newsboy around there—he lent me the money. I cleaned that little horn out, scaled it good. It was all right. Made a little living with it.

"Later," Louis continued, "when I was playing in Henry Matranga's honky-tonk, Joe Oliver used to come around after Peta Lala's closed down in the district, and he'd say, 'I'm sick of looking at that beat-up cornet. I'm going to give you a horn.' So one night he gave me an old York he'd had. Oh, my! I drooled all over the place. 'Thanks, Papa Joe, thank you Mister Joe.' I always knew, if I'm going to get a little break in this game, it was going to be through Papa Joe, nobody else. He used to have me to his house to eat red beans and rice . . . He gave me lessons out of an exercise book— then we'd run down little duets together."

After Louis had been living with his father and step-mother awhile, a new addition came to the family: little Gertrude. Even with both parents working, the burden of four children to support was more than they could handle. One night Mayann came to visit, and Willie took her aside for a private talk. When they came back, they asked Louis if he wanted to live with his mother again.

He was delighted, although there was a tinge of sadness in this parting, as well. He had learned to love his father and Gertrude, and little Henry, although he could have lived quite well without little Willie. He said yes and went with Mayann that very evening. As he left, he promised to return often for a visit to his other family.

In *My Life in New Orleans,* Louis said that the morning after he came back to Perdido and Liberty Streets, he went out looking for his old friends. The first person he ran into was Cocaine Buddy Martin. Earlier, Louis had romanced Cocaine Buddy's sister, Bela. Buddy didn't know that Louis had been released from the Home.

Buddy had grown since Louis last saw him, now wore long pants. He worked for Joe Segretta, who ran a combination grocery, saloon and honky-tonk. Across the street from Segretta's was Henry Ponce's honky-tonk. Ponce was one of the biggest operators in the district; a Frenchman, Segretta was an Italian. The two were bitter enemies, although Louis did not know that at the time. Both were tough characters, who tried to show one another up at every chance.

There was a job in Ponce's, playing the blues for the whores who came in with large rolls of dollar bills tucked into the top of their stockings. Weeknights, the honky-tonk stayed open till four in the morning; Saturdays, all night. Louis never got home before ten or eleven, Sunday morning. Buddy put in a good word for him with Ponce, and he got the job. Mayann fixed him a bucket-lunch, to save having to eat at the lunch counters and lunch wagons.

Louis was young, strong for his size, and ambitious. Many of the musicians had a second job during the day, because the honky-tonks could be closed down at any time. When Ponce's closed for the night, Louis hurried home for two hours of sleep, then got up at six to report to the C. A. Andrews Coal Company at Ferret and Perdido. He hauled hard coal from seven in the morning until five in the evening, shoveling a ton of coal into his wagon each trip. It was back-breaking labor, although made easier by tips from his stepfather, Gabe, who worked steadily at the coal yard.

Gabe drove a wagon with two mules, and made thirty cents a load; he could deliver nine or ten loads a day. As small as Louis was, he could make no more than five trips a day, earning fifteen cents a load, or seventy-five cents a day. That, plus the dollar and a quarter and tips from the honky-tonk, was good money.

Louis tried time and again to talk Mayann into taking Gabe back, but she had set her mind against him. Gabe remained Louis' favorite among his many stepfathers.

Times were good, for a while. Then, during an election campaign, the honky-tonks were closed down by the police. Henry Ponce intended to reopen as soon as things cooled down, but the crackdown lasted so long that he got discouraged and went into a more legitimate business downtown.

For a time, Lous could go straight home after his job ended on the coal cart. However, after supper he usually dressed up in his tailor-made long pants, for which he had saved for some time, and went out to make the rounds of the honky-tonks with his friend, Isaac "Ike"

Smooth. Ike had been in the Home and in the Home's band with him.

Their main pleasure in life was listening to the music, although they laughed at the drunks. The honky-tonks usually had three rooms: the first was the saloon, the second for gambling. The preferred game was cotch, with three cards dealt off the bottom. High card won. Louis sometimes scraped up his nickels to play, but his face was transparent whenever he got a good hand. Thus he never won.

The third room in the honky-tonk was for dancing, usually with a small bandstand catty-cornered at the end of the room. The bands frequently had no more than three pieces. Some that Louis played with had piano, drums and his cornet. The Battlefield was the playground for dozens of fascinating characters: the whores, and their pimps and the gamblers. Among them was Black Benny, the musicians' friend. He was about ten years older than Louis and as tough as they came. Any time toughs gave the musicians a hard time, Benny took care of them.

Benny was constantly in trouble with the law, although he never served more than thirty days at a time. He was also one of the best drummers ever to play in the brass bands. Whenever the bands had to play for a funeral, they would ask the police to let Benny out long enough to finish the gig. As soon as the funeral was over, Benny went back to jail. His arrests were always for fighting or for beating the hell out of his girl, Nelly—never for stealing.

At the time it seemed as though all of Louis' friends were pimping a girl, so he decided to find one of his own. The girl he chose was short, nappy-haired and cursed with buck teeth; but she made what seemed like good money to Louis. Their relationship was strictly a business one, but one night she insisted that he go home with her.

At that time, Louis was still shy with women; and except for his term at the Home, he had never spent a night away from his family. He resisted the girl's advances until she pulled a pocketknife. Before Louis knew what was happening, she stabbed him in the left shoulder.

The blood ran down his back. Frightened, Louis headed for home, afraid to tell Mayann what had happened. But she saw the blood on his back and made him confess the truth. Then she headed straight for the girl's house and knocked on the door while the girl was getting ready for bed.

When she opened the door Mayann grabbed her by the throat and began to choke her. "What you stab my son for?"

Mayann was a big woman, and strong. She threw the girl on the floor and jumped on her, but before she could kill her, Black Benny and some of the other men heard the commotion and came rushing in.

"Don't kill her, Mayann!" shouted Benny. "She won't do it again!"

Mayann let the girl get up, and warned her to stay way from Louis. The warning was unnecessary. Louis had learned his lesson and never went near her again.

Arthur Brown had been one of Louis' playmates, and was one of the most popular boys in the district. Arthur was going with a girl who had a little brother; the brother was always playing with a knife or a pistol. One day he pointed the pistol at Arthur and pulled the trigger; Arthur fell dead.

All of the young people chipped in to hire the Onward Brass Band to play for the funeral. The band was per-

haps the best of the marching bands available: Joe
Oliver and Emanuel Perez played the cornets, Eddy
Jackson the bass tuba, and Black Benny the bass drum.
The pallbearers were Louis, Cocaine Buddy, Little
Head Lucas, Egg Head Papa and Harry Tennisen.

Everybody cried at the funeral. Later that year, Harry
Tennisen was killed by a girl named Sister Pop, shot in
the brain with a .45. Later on, both Lucas and Cocaine
Buddy died of tuberculosis.

Wakes and funerals were a popular form of entertainment. There was one man, called Sweet Child, who attended very wake in town, whether or not he knew the
deceased. Sweet Child usually led off the singing with a
hymn. His clothes weren't very good, and usually didn't
match; but they were always pressed, and his shoes were
always shined.

Later, when Louis began to play in the brass bands
with men like Joe Oliver, Roy Palmer, Sam Dutrey and
his brother, Honore, Oscar Celestine, Oak Gasper,
Buddy Petit, Kid Ory, Mutt Carey and his brother,
Jack, he saw Sweet Child at every funeral.

For a time, funerals were the only chance Louis had
to play his cornet. The War had started, and a draft law
had been passed. He was willing to join the army, but he
was only seventeen. At that time, the army was taking
only men twenty-one and older. He tried to enlist in the
navy, lying about his age, but they checked up on his
birth certificate and turned him down.

The coal wagon was not Louis' favorite way to make
a living. Every time a hustle came along that seemed to
offer an easier dollar, he changed jobs. For a time he
worked unloading the banana boats, until a big rat
jumped out of the bunch he was carrying to the checker.
Louis dropped the bunch and started running. He didn't

stop until he was safe at home. For the rest of his life he was unable to eat a banana, although before the incident he was fond of them.

One job was as a helper on a milk wagon, delivering to the West End and the summer resorts at Spanish Fort. The roads there were made of crushed oyster shells. One Sunday morning Louis jumped on the wagon while it was moving and slipped under the wheel. The wagon ran over his foot, tore open the top of his big toe; sharp pieces of shell were driven into the wound.

The milkman drove him to the Charity Hospital, miles away in New Orleans. At the hospital, the doctors asked if he was going to sue the milk company, but he said no, the accident had been his own fault.

Mayann fainted when Louis came home with his bandaged foot, but when her friends pressed her to sue the milk company, she refused. The decision was Louis' to make, and he had made it.

Boys who worked on the milk wagons were paid off about ten o'clock Friday mornings. They usually went around the corner to shoot craps. Unlucky at cards, the dice were another matter. Frequently Louis came home from the games with his pockets stuffed with money. At last Mayann became frightened that he was doing something wrong and demanded to know where he got it.

Expecting a whipping, Louis told her the truth. Instead, Mayann reminded him how hard it had been to get him released from the Home. By then, any regrets at leaving the Home had long been forgotten. Louis promptly went down to Canal Street and blew his winnings on new clothes for his family, new pants for himself. There wasn't enough money for new shoes, so he went barefoot, as usual.

After the accident Louis returned to the milk company; but business fell off, and both the driver and Louis were laid off. For a while there was no work, until the government opened up a war construction job. Many well-known musicians took jobs there, including Kid Ory, who was a carpenter by trade. Louis was proud of the big yellow identification badge that gave him entrance to the job.

When that job closed down, for a time he worked for a wrecking company. The other men at the wreckers told him stories of finding money and treasure in the old houses they tore down, and the company rule was finders, keepers. Louis tore into each new job with a fury, but the treasures eluded him.

From there, he had a job with Ike Smooth's father, whitewashing buildings. Another time he worked as a dishwasher in Thompson's Restaurant, at Canal and Rampart Streets. On that job he was permitted to eat all of the cream puffs, doughnuts and ice cream that he wanted. For two weeks he gorged on sweets, until the very sight of rich desserts made him ill. He quit the restaurant, went back to the coal yard; and while there, wrote *Coal Cart Blues*, which he recorded years later.

It was during those years that Mama Lucy went to Florida to work. There was a shortage of laborers in Florida, and a sawmill had put an advertisement in a New Orleans newspaper. Mama Lucy was a big, brassy teenager. At home, she hung out with cousin Flora Miles, but after Mama Lucy left, Flora began hanging out with another crowd. With them, she got into the family way.

The father was a white man, an old man who lived in a ramshackle house and was known for enticing young colored girls into his home. The baby was born, a boy named Clarence. The adults in the district tried to have

Ike Miles bring charges against the white man, but Ike knew better. It would have been futile at best; at worst, they were apt to find themselves out into the street, if not into jail.

At the time Clarence was born, Louis was the only one in the family making a decent wage. He sold newspapers on the street and played his cornet on the side. Supporting the baby fell to him. Times were getting worse. Frequently Louis went down to the produce houses in the French Quarter where the spoiled vegetables and poultry were thrown into big barrels for the garbage wagons to haul away.

He pulled out the best of the discards: half-spoiled chickens, turkeys, ducks and geese. At home, Mayann cut out the bad parts and boiled the good parts thoroughly. They then dressed them nicely and put the food into baskets, and Louis sold them to fine restaurants. Usually the owner of the restaurant paid a decent price and threw in a good meal or a few sandwiches to boot.

They did the same with potatoes, cutting out the bad parts and selling the good for six bits a sack. Sometimes Louis followed the garbage wagons to the Silver City dump, where an army of poor blacks waited with pokers to pick through the trash. Sometimes they found whole pork chops and unspoiled loaves of bread, even good clothing that had been discarded by white families.

The day Clarence was born, a hurricane hit New Orleans—one of the worst storms the city had ever seen. Houses were blown down and people and animals were killed. Thousands were left homeless. Louis was in the street, on his way home, when the hurricane struck. Slates were torn off the rooftops and blown into the streets, falling all around him. He should have sought shelter, but he was so worried about his family that he struggled on, and at last reached home safely.

Casualties were high all across the city. Musicians such as Joe Oliver, Bunk Johnson, Freddie Keppard and Henry Allen, all trumpet players, made a lot of money playing at funerals of slain lodge members.

Flora Miles finally died, after first changing the baby's name to Clarence Armstrong. Louis took care of the boy from that time, formally adopting him when he lived in Chicago with his second wife, Lil Hardin. Unfortunately, Clarence was retarded, but Louis showered him with affection from the time he was a baby.

In *My Life in New Orleans*, Louis said that this was when he started working with Morris Karnofsky on the coal cart, selling stone coal to the girls in Storyville. Apparently Louis could pass for being younger than his actual age. He used the opportunity to sneak into Pete Lala's cabaret in the red light district, where Joe Oliver was playing. Others in the Oliver band were drummer Harry Zeno, Buddy Christian, doubling on guitar and piano, Zue Robertson on trombone, Jimmy Noone on clarinet, and Bob Lyons on bass violin. Between 1910 and 1917, the Oliver band was the hottest in New Orleans. Most musicians doubled, playing with one group in the honky-tonks and with others in the brass bands.

Along about this time Louis formed a little orchestra of his own, with his friend Joe Lindsey. Joe was a good drummer; they added Morris French on the trombone and Louis Prevott on the clarinet. There were only six pieces, bass violin and guitar added to the horns. Like other bands, they accepted whatever gigs came along, including the Saturday advertising wagons.

Louis said later that his band was second best in the

city, after the band that included Joe Oliver and Kid Ory. They fought in their share of cutting contests, but Oliver told Louis to stand up when their paths crossed, so he would recognize him and not try to carve him up. When that happened, Joe Oliver stood up in his wagon and played a few short pieces, then moved on.

One time they met, but Louis forgot to stand. The Oliver-Ory band proceeded to tear them apart. The boys felt unhappy, but accepted it as good sports. They knew when they had met the masters.

Joe Oliver was almost a second father to Louis. He ran errands for Joe's wife, Stella, and Joe gave him the lessons previously mentioned as his pay. Some already-famous musicians, such as Jelly Roll Morton and Freddie Keppard had already moved north, long before Storyville was closed down by the navy.

By then Louis had gotten over his earlier shyness with girls. He was playing in a honky-tonk with Sonny Garber on the drums and a man known as Boogus on the piano, when his eye fell on a girl, sitting alone. Later he discovered that she had just arrived from Memphis, and knew no one in New Orleans. Louis didn't speak to her that night, but she returned several days in a row. By that time she had gotten mixed up with a local gambler named Cheeky Black.

One morning, during intermission, Louis sat down and introduced himself. He learned that her name was Irene, and that Cheeky Black had taken all of her money; she hadn't eaten in two days. Louis was a soft touch, then and throughout the rest of his life. He gave her most of his salary and when Cheeky finally went on his way, moved in with her.

Louis was just seventeen; he was also in love. Irene was twenty-one. He expected Mayann to raise objections, but she felt he was old enough to live his life as he chose.

They lived together as man and wife; but one day Irene became very sick, suffering from stomach pains. At night she groaned constantly, until Louis didn't know what to do. Money was very short at the time, and he couldn't afford a doctor. Then he met Joe Oliver on the street, and told him, sadly, about Irene.

"You need money for a doctor?" said Oliver. "Go down and take my place at Pete Lala's for two nights."

Joe Oliver was making top money—a dollar and a half a night, plus very good tips. In two nights Louis could make all that he needed. It had also been some time since he had a chance to earn money with his horn.

He accepted the offer with thanks, but when the time came to show up for work, Louis was frightened. Lala came over when he took his place with the band, demanding to know who he was and what had happened to Oliver. Louis explained that Joe had sent him to take his place for two nights.

To his surprise, Lala let him play. The honky-tonk owner had a club foot, which he dragged when he walked. Every few minutes he dragged that foot over to the bandstand, to say, "Boy, keep that bute in your horn!"

It wasn't until the end of the evening that Louis understood what Lala meant: he wanted him to keep the mute in his horn. When the honky-tonk closed for the night Lala told him not to come back again; but Joe Oliver paid him for both nights anyway.

1917 proved to be an important year for Louis. Joe Lindsey met an older woman who made him quit the band, which then broke up. The next time Louis saw Joe, he had married the woman and was working as a chaffeur. The time after that, the woman had thrown him over.

Louis realized that the difference in ages meant a great deal; he told Irene that she'd be better off with someone older. However, age difference meant nothing a year later, when he fell in love again and this time married the girl.

Louis left New Orleans for a time, taking a job playing with a little band in the small town of Houma. The band was owned by the undertaker, a Mr. Bonds, who paid Louis a weekly salary. Louis took his meals with the family in their home, which was the funeral parlor. He stayed in Houma longer than he had intended, and when he returned to the city, Irene was gone.

One day, with no work in sight, several of the boys were hanging around together when one came up with the idea of hopping the freight tran and migrating about the countryside to take jobs on the sugar cane plantations. Louis went along, not taking time to tell Mayann goodbye.

They got to Harrihan, about thirty miles from the city, just about the time Louis began to get hungry. The hungrier he got, the more he thought about Mayann's cooking, and the spaghetti and meatballs she had been fixing when he left that morning. Finally his stomach told him to jump off the freight and catch the next train heading back.

He reached home just in time for supper, sat down and dug in. He never told Mayann about his adventure.

Thanks to the war, things were getting tougher; and just about then, a serious flu epidemic struck the city. Everybody came down with it, except Louis. His luck in escaping the virus he later ascribed to his weekly psychic.

For a time all public enfertainments were closed down. Just when it seemed the epidemic was easing, the flu struck again, harder than before. But at last Louis found work in a third-rate honky-tonk the law hadn't bothered to shut down.

Henry Matranga was Louis' new boss, and Matranga was a good man to work for. At the time, Mayann worked in Matranga's home. Whenever Louis dropped by at mealtime to visit his mother, he was made to sit down at the kitchen table and given a plate of their good spaghetti.

Matranga left the funning of the place to Slippers, his black bouncer. Slippers had suggested Louis as a replacement for the cornet player who had left. The honky-tonks were frequently raided by the police—the customers and the employees hauled down to the jail. This, and other arrests, happened so many times over the years that Louis lived and played in New Orleans that he lost track of the number. In a letter to Max Jones, he said:

"When I married Daisy (my first wife) she was a prostitute from across the river. . .She was twenty-one years old and I was eighteen. . .And the way those tough men such as gamblers; pimps, etc., got along with their wives and whores, that was the same way that I had to get along with Daisy. That was to beat the hell out of her every night and make love in order to get some sleep. . .many times she and I went to jail from fighting in the streets, and my boss would have to come get me out. Now you can see why I don't remember just how many times that I went to jail. It was a common thing in those days. I can proudly say though that I didn't steal—much. I didn't have to. . ."

When Louis was arrested on the job, he stayed there until Matranga made bail for them all. Sometimes they stayed a few days, rarely as much as nineteen or twenty.

One day he ran into Irene on the street. He hadn't seen her for some time, and she didn't tell Louis that she had gone back to Cheeky Black. She invited him home, and he went along. They were just about to doze off to sleep when the doorknob rattled.

Louis had locked the door, but a moment later Cheeky came bursting into the room, waving his razor. Irene screamed, and ran almost naked to the street. Cheeky chased her, leaving Louis to struggle into his clothes. He could hear people trying to calm Cheeky down. Louis ran out and straight home to Mayann, rushing into the house out of breath.

"So you've been in another man's house with his old lady?" said Mayann, laughing. "This will teach you a lesson."

It did, although Mayann made herself almost sick with laughter. She told Louis she would straighten out matters with Cheeky. After all, Irene should never have invited him home while she was living with another man. After that, Louis was just as happy that he never saw Irene again.

1918 arrived, and things began to look up. For a time Louis took a job as a bellboy for the saloon on his corner, replacing Sweet Child. His job was to walk along the street until one of the whores stuck her head out of the window to yell: "Bellyboy! Bring me half a can!"

Half a can was a nickel's worth of beer; a whole can was a dime's worth. Half a can was so much that sometimes it was necessary to have a neighbor share in finishing it up. Louis enjoyed going into the houses. Sometimes, when the girls couldn't afford even half a can, he bought it for them out of his tips.

One day Sweet Child came back, and Louis went back to the coal yard with Gabe. Then, along about the middle of summer, Joe Oliver got an offer to go north, to play at the Lincoln Gardens in Chicago.

Going north meant hitting the big time. Every musician in New Orleans dreamed of going to Chicago. Jazz had moved up the Mississippi, first to St. Paul with the riverboats, and from there to Chicago.

Louis took time off from the coal cart to see his friend leave on the train. Oliver was taking Jimmy Noone, his clarinet player, with him. Kid Ory was also at the station, with the band, to say good-bye.

The parting was sorrowful, for Louis knew that he would miss Joe and Stella Oliver. As soon as the train pulled out he headed back for his cart; then Kid Ory called after him.

"You still blowin' that cornet?"

Louis stopped, then turned and ran back. When the boys in the band heard that Oliver was definitely leaving, they had told Ory to get Little Louis as his replacement. Ory knew Louis' playing, but he looked around town first, trying to find someone with more experience. But after Oliver, Louis was the best man around.

He offered the job to Louis. After years of playing with amateur talent and in the cheapest honky-tonks, Louis had his chance at the very top.

6
MARRIAGE AND THE RIVER

6

Marriage and the River

When Louis started with Kid Ory he kept the job with
the coal yard. The draft age had been extended from
eighteen to forty-five, and the rule was work or serve.
Louis had registered, but apparently his earlier fervor
for the War had cooled considerably.

It was about then that Sidney Bechet came uptown
from the Creole quarter to play clarinet at Kid Brown's
honky-tonk, at Gravier and Franklin. The first time
Louis heard Bechet's music, he knew that here was
someone special. That Labor Day every band in town
was playing in the big parade, but for some reason
Bechet had no gig. The more famous Henry Allen, Red
Allen's father, was playing for one of the social clubs
when he spotted the young Bechet.

Short a cornet, he sent Bechet to borrow one from

Bob Lyons, the bass player. Bechet was as good on the cornet as he was on the clarinet, blowing up a storm. Louis said he outplayed everybody else in town that day.

Once Louis and Bechet had the chance to play together, on one of the advertising wagons. Besides their horns, there was a drummer. A short time later Bechet moved north, and then he went to Europe, where he became one of the most famous musicians of his day.

After Kid Ory hired Louis, he headed straight for home to give Mayann the good news. Louis had studied Ory's band closely, and knew almost all of their numbers. When he played with them, he tried to emulate Joe Oliver, to the point of wrapping a bath towel around his neck when the band played a ball at Economy Hall. That had been Oliver's trademark.

Anything Louis didn't know, his talented ear quickly picked up; he became known for his quickness. Kid Ory was a patient man and pleased with his new cornet player. The band was already a favorite with the dance audiences, and Louis soon earned the same loyalty. Other musicians began showing up, just to listen to the music. When Louis had a night off, he was beseiged with offers to play with other groups.

The Dutrey brothers were among the best musicians in town: Sam on the clarinet, and Honore on the trombone. Honore later played with Louis' band in Chicago, in 1926, but first he served a hitch in the navy, during which he once fell asleep in a powder magazine. While he slept, he gassed himself so badly that for the rest of his life he suffered terribly from asthma. Honore's reduced lung capacity affected his ability to play the upper register, but he was still one of the best in the lower ranges.

Kid Ory played some of the finest gigs in town, especially for the whites. The band often played dances at the Country Club, which was one of Louis' favorites. During intermission, the waiters fed the musicians the same meal as the paying customers received. Louis and the drummer made friends with the waiters, and were able to take food home to their familes.

Robechaux's brass band was good, but the musicians in it considered themselves better than Ory's men because they could read music. One day Robechaux was supposed to play for a funeral, but a number of his men had to work. He asked Ory to fill out the group.

The Ory men played all of the music they were given without trouble, but Robechaux's men still had their noses in the air. After the body was in the grave, however, the band swung into a ragtime march. Ory's blows blew the music readers almost out of their shoes. The second line made them take an encore, something that almost never happened in funeral parades.

The band marched into the lodge hall, swinging on *Panama*, and Louis playing up in the high registers. Robechaux conceded defeat; and after that hired them several times. Finally he asked the men Ory let him borrow to join his group. But Louis had already given Oscar Celestin his promise that he'd join Celestin's Tuxedo Brass Band, replacing another top cornet man, Sidney Desvigne. After the Onward Brass Band, with Joe Oliver and Emmanuel Perez, broke up, the Tuxedo Brass Band was the undisputed best in town.

Armistice Day of 1918 was the last day Louis worked on the coal chart. At eleven that morning he was unloading coal at Fabacher's restaurant on St. Charles Street. Fabacher's was one of the finest restaurants of the day. He heard a string of autos making an ungodly racket, tin cans tied to their bumpers. Asking what was happening, somebody said the war was over.

Louis put about three more shovels of coal into the wheelbarrow, and then he stopped. He thought a minute, then put on his jacket. Looked at Lady, the mule hitched to the coal cart, and said good-bye.

He cut for home, leaving mule cart, coal, and everything connected with the job standing in front of the restaurant. He never saw mule nor cart nor coal again.

The next day the lights came on all over town, for the first time in more than a year. All of the places that had been closed for austerity reasons suddenly reopened. Matranga offered Louis his old job, but Louis was looking forward to better things.

Kid Ory suddenly had more gigs than he could handle. He even began holding his own dances, Monday nights at the Economy Hall. Mondays were normally the slowest night of the week, but the dances were immediately successful. Ory prospered, and with him, the band.

Most Saturdays, however, the band was idle. On those nights Louis took a job at the Brick House, across the river in Gretna. The Brick House was a honky-tonk, and attracted a rough crowd. A careless person could find himself with his head blown off or cut off.

But the tips were good. There were only three pieces in the band, and the whores demanded they play almost nothing but the blues. The blues were popular all over the South at that time. When the whores and the hustlers got into their cups, they became maudlin.

The Brick House was located next to the levee, by the Jackson Avenue ferry. When the honky-tonk closed late at night, Louis used to worry about going home. There were tense moments between the white and the colored drunks. Saturdays, the levee workers came into the honky-tonk to make dates with the girls, and to drink and to fight. Cuttings and shootings were frequent, and sometimes bottles came flying over the bandstand.

Louis was lucky, however; he survived. But he noticed one girl among the others, a regular. Three Saturdays in a row she gave him the eye before he struck up an acquaintance during an intermission.

That was his first meeting with Daisy Parker. It was only natural that one night he follow her upstairs, in a business arrangement. Daisy's price seemed reasonable, but that first time they stayed together from five in the morning until well into the afternoon.

Daisy was a good-looking woman, until she took off her clothes. The preference in those days was for girls with a certain amount of meat on their bones; but Daisy was skinny. She weighed less than a hundred pounds. The first time they were along, Louis found out that she had been wearing a pair of "sides"—artificial hips—to give herself a more bountiful shape.

The padding did not put him off, and there were several similar meetings after that. It was perhaps inevitable that they fall in love, for Louis had that problem time and again over the next twenty years. After Irene, Daisy marked his second fling with that emotion.

He didn't know until later that Daisy had an old man, a common-law husband. Daisy's old man was a drummer who worked in another honky-tonk in Gretna. They lived together in Freetown, a village between Gretna and Algiers.

Daisy kept extending invitations for Louis to visit her some afternoon when he wasn't working. Then Kid Ory signed a contract to play every Saturday night at the New Orleans Country Club.

Louis quit the Brick House, and for the next month did not see Daisy, although from time to time they talked on the telephone. Then one day he decided to cross the river and pay her the long-postponed visit. He put on his one good suit and his best shoes and his good hat.

After the ferry, he had to take a bus that let him out almost a mile from Daisy's door. She lived in a four-room house, the rooms one behind the other, like a rail-road flat. The house was old and in poor condition. Daisy greeted him with a smile and led him into the parlor, where they kissed like long-lost lovers.

No sooner had Daisy settled into Louis' lap when there came a rap on the door, and her old man came in. Perhaps Louis remembered the encounter with Cheeky Black. He jumped into his clothes while Daisy ran into the next room, her man close on her heels. Then Louis heard something hit the floor.

Daisy had been knocked out with one blow of her man's fist. Louis grabbed his hat from the sewing machine and lit out in a dead run. He held onto his hat until he was safe on the ferry, for it was common know-ledge that hats could slow a serious runner down. The running he did that afternoon was as serious as any Louis did in his life.

Another month passed. Louis had decided that Daisy was more trouble than she was worth. Then one day, while he was standing on the corner with men who had just come from the coalyards, she showed up. Daisy had been looking for him, and she ran to him and kissed him.

His friends were impressed that Louis had himself such a good-looking woman, and he was happy to be able to show off in front of them. He took Daisy to Kid

Green's hotel, at Rampart and Lafayette Streets. Kid Green was a retired prizefighter and one of Louis' admirers. His hotel wasn't much, but it was comfortable; and he always managed to find a room for Louis and his dates, no matter how crowded he might be. Apparently that happened quite often.

Kid Green gave them a room that day to talk, and Louis grilled Daisy on her past. He found out that she had been spoiled by her parents, and that she was extremely jealous. Later he discovered that she could neither read nor write; but she was a master at fussing and fighting.

Nonetheless, he was in love. When they left the hotel, their destination was city hall. There was no waiting period for marriages in those days; they were married by an official that same day.

Louis' friends spotted Daisy for what she was, and made a beeline to Mayann to ask if she was going to let him marry that whore. Mayann shrugged. Louis was old enough at eighteen to live his own life. If he was really in love, the marriage had her blessing.

For the next month the newlyweds met at different hotels or wherever they could get together; they lacked the money to set up housekeeping. At last Louis found a two-room flat he could afford Uptown, on Melpomine Street. It was over an upholsterer's shop, and in bad condition. The alley behind the shop stank from years of accumulated garbage, but the only entrance to the flat was by an outside stairs that came up from the alley.

It wasn't much, but it was home. Clarence was about three at the time, and Louis took the boy to live with them. One of Louis' first luxury purchases was a wind-up Victrola, and one rainy day he and Daisy were listenng to some new records, releases of the Original Dixieland Jazz Band. In *My Life in New Orleans*, he remembered that the records were *Livery Stable Blues* and the first *Tiger Rag* ever recorded.

Clarence was playing on the back gallery, which is what New Orleans residents call the porch. Suddenly Louis heard the boy cry out. He had slipped off the gallery, fallen to the ground.

The fall apparently caused the boy's retardation. Louis took Clarence to the best doctors he could find, and later enrolled him in the best schools, including a Catholic school. But the doctors of the time were unable to do anything for the boy. At last Louis took over Clarence's training himself, taught him to get along in society. However, he was never able to work, or to support himself.

To earn extra money while married to Daisy, Louis used to visit the charcoal schooners tied up at the head of the New Basin Canal. The men on the schooners cleaned out the largest lumps of charcoal and sacked them, but the small pieces weren't considered desirable. The latter were thrown into a corner. Louis, and others like him, bought the little pieces for a small sum and carried them away in big burlap sacks. At home, he packed the charcoal in water buckets and sold it house to house at five cents a bucket

Whenever Daisy was in a mood to fight, and that was often, Louis packed his and Clarence's clothes into the charcoal sack and moved back with Mayann. Every time he left, he swore that this time he wouldn't return to Daisy. She always came after him, filled with apologies and promises not to upset him, or annoy him while he was trying to practice with his horn.

Living in the neighborhood was one of Louis' former

girl friends, Rella Martin. Somehow Daisy found out about Rella; and every time he was as much as half an hour late, she started another fight, accusing him of being with Rella. His protestations of innocence were of no avail.

Then a member of Louis' social club, The Tammany Social Aid and Pleasure Club, died. Louis got his black broadcloth suit out of pawn in time for the funeral. While the body was still in the church, he stood on the corner, talking to Rella and Little Head Lucas.

It had been raining all morning. The gutters were full and the streets were muddy. Louis had a brand new Stetson hat and new patent-leather shoes. The hat was the mark of a successful man. Stetsons cost fifteen dollars in those days, and men saved their pennies for months. There was no greater proof of pride than to be seen wearing the newest and the sharpest hat.

Louis spotted Daisy headed in his direction. He told the others, and Rella took off. As Daisy came up she started cursing Louis and calling him names; and then she pulled out her razor.

Louis took off without wanting to argue any further; but as he jumped the gutter he lost his hat. Little Head started to pick it up for him, but Daisy made a swipe toward him with the razor. Little Head took off, past Louis.

Daisy then picked up the hat and started slashing it to ribbons. That made Louis so mad he turned and started back for her; but some of the other club members grabbed him and held him back. Then Daisy threw the wreck of the hat into the mud and took off for downtown.

The body was about to come out; Louis had to take his place in the line. The cemetery was close to where he lived with Daisy, and as soon as the body was in the grave, he started for home.

Daisy was not in the flat. Instead, she was hiding with a friend upstairs. First, however, she had accumulated a pile of bricks.

Just as Louis put his key in the lock, the bricks began to fly. He did his best to duck until her ammunition ran out, and then Daisy came flying down the stairs. Louis grabbed one of the bricks and threw it back. The missile caught her her in the stomach, and she doubled over, screaming: "You've killed me! You've killed me!"

Louis didn't wait to hear anything else Daisy might say. Someone had already called the cops, and when he heard the patrol bell, he vaulted for the back fence.

Daisy was hauled off to jail, screaming and cursing. While the police were trying to get her into the patrol wagon, she kicked one of them under the chin. In retaliation, he hit her with his night stick, opening a bad cut. But when she got to the jail, Daisy knew better than to report him. All the way to the jail she carried on, crying as though she were an innocent babe.

In the meantime, Louis had caught up with the funeral parade again and borrowed another good Stetson from a good friend among the bystanders. While he was marching back to the club, word came that Daisy was in jail, although the cops hadn't booked her. He sent back word for her not to worry, that all was forgiven.

As soon as the funeral parade ended, Louis made a line for the corner grocery and called his boss on the telephone. Few blacks could afford phones in those days, and the corner grocery was the lifeline for almost everyone. Some telephone companies used to offer a special class of service when it was necessary to have the wanted party summoned from another place to the phone.

Louis' boss called the station, and Daisy was released. Louis met her at the station, Daisy limping when she came out. But they kissed and made up. As they walked home, however, she began to get angry all over again. She turned on Louis and began to curse him, saying that he had crippled her for life but she'd get her revenge.

The fight continued all the way home. Louis belted her a few times. Near the flat they met a policeman who had the reputation of being the toughest cop in the city. But he knew Louis from his playing with Kid Ory, and instead of throwing them back into jail for fighting, he warned Louis to get Daisy off the street.

Louis decided it was time to have a heart to heart talk with his wife. Every time they fought, Daisy's first move was to try and hit him in the chops. If she ever connected, he wouldn't be able to play his horn.

He told her it was time to call it quits. Daisy broke into tears, begged Louis not to leave her. Against his better judgment, they made up once more, and toughed it out together a while longer. His marriage to Daisy was to last through four tumultuous years, with many separations and almost constant fighting, until finally Louis left New Orleans to join Joe Oliver in Chicago.

One day while he was engaged in a cutting contest with another advertising wagon, a stranger stopped to listen. Louis had already received many offers to leave Kid Ory, but until then none had been really tempting. Fletcher Henderson had written from New York, asking Louis to join his famous orchestra.

Louis had said time and again that he would leave New Orleans only if Papa Joe Oliver sent for him, but the Henderson offer was almost too good to resist. He talked it over with his close friend, Zutty Singleton. The upshot was that he wrote back to say that if Henderson had a spot for Zutty, a drummer, then both would come.

Fletcher Henderson, unfortunately, had no need of another drummer. Five years were to pass before the invitation was extended again.

The stranger was Fate Marable. Marable had been playing on the excursion steamer *Sydney* for more than sixteen years, and was one of the best piano men around. He also played the calliope on the top deck as the steamer left the docks for one of its moonlight trips up the Mississippi.

Marable's offer meant a great advance in Louis' career. He accepted immediately. But Fate Marable's musicians had to be able to read music, which none of Kid Ory's men could do. For that reason the Marable orchestra could improvise on the latest songs from a sight reading of the sheet music, while Ory had to wait until he heard the song played by another band before he could pick up on it.

Louis joined the Marable band right away. In the orchestra, playing the mellophone, was David Jones. Jones took an interest in Louis and between trips taught him how to read and how to divide the notes so that he could cope with any new arrangements that Fate might give them.

Marable had been aware that Louis could not read music, but he liked his tone and Louis' quick ear. The orchestra leader liked to throw hard pieces at his men to catch them off guard, scanning his own part in advance. Then the members of the band scrambled to read their parts when he passed them around.

Fate was respected by every musician in New Orleans. At one time or another he had played with all greats of his day, holding his own and frequently winning honors. If one of his band made a mistake, he said nothing about it until the next day. If you came to work with a hangover, he handed you the music where you had made the mistake and asked you to play it alone. Louis soon learned from that object lesson.

At the time Louis joined the band, the *Sydney* was making evening excursions that started about 8:30 and returned to New Orleans at midnight. After his night with the band, Louis hurried home to tell Daisy about his experience. Instead of being happy for him, however, she was afraid that he would leave her.

Besides David Jones, in the Marable band were Joe Howard as first cornet, Baby Dodds on drums, George (Pops) Foster on bass, Johnny St. Cyr on banjo and guitar, Boyd Atkings on swing violin, and another, whose name Louis later could not recall.

The *Sydney* was a rear-wheeler, one of three Mississippi steamers owned by the Streckfus company. The company was owned by four brothers: Vern, Roy, Johnny and Joe. Captain Joe was the oldest, and boss. Captain Vern reminded Louis of his favorite comedian, Stan Laurel.

The other two Streckfus boats, the *J.S.* and the *St. Paul*, were sidewheelers. After Louis worked on the *Sydney* for a time, he was told the boat was about to leave New Orleans on an extended trip upriver, where it would stop and run excursions for the many small towns along the way.

During the last week before he left home, Louis met a young white boy who later would become very important to him. Jack Teagarden remembered his first introduction to Louis in an interview in the December 1944 *Esquire*:

"In the small hours, a friend and I were wandering around the French Quarter, when suddenly I heard trumpet in the distance. I couldn't see anything but an excursion boat gliding through the mist back to port. Then the tune became more distinct. The boat was still far off. But in the bow I could see a Negro standing in the wind, holding a trumpet high and sending out the most brilliant notes I had ever heard. It was jazz; it was what I had been hoping to hear all through the night. I don't even know whether it was *Tiger Rag* or *Panama*. But it was Louis Armstrong descending from the sky like a god. The ship hugged the bank as if it were driven there by the powerful trumpet beats. I stayed absolutely still, just listening, until the boat dropped anchor. It was Fate Marable's orchestra. Gene Sedric played the saxophone. I talked with the musicians when they landed and Fate Marable presented me to the unknown cornetist with the round open face: Louis Armstrong!"

Louis' own thoughts on first hearing Teagarden's trombone are not recorded, but he said later that it was a memorable occasion. However, several years were to pass before they met again and joined forces.

The Marable band was the first colored band to play most of the small towns at which they stopped, breaking the Jim Crow barriers. There were ugly experiences and nasty remarks, but the musicians were used to such comments from the whites in New Orleans. They kept playing as though nothing had happened, and before the evening finished the crowd always swung around to their side.

When Louis joined Marable, he weighed only 140 pounds. One day he caught a bad cold, and David Jones recommended he get a bottle of Scott's Emulsion and take it regularly until it was gone. Within a week Louis began to gain weight, and from that time he remained heavy. In later years his weight ranged from 180 to more than 220.

Once they were on the river, the day excursions lasted all day long. The second year Louis worked the other boats, joining the band in St. Louis. That gave him his first real train ride. (Hopping the freights didn't count.)

Each spring the band traveled to Davenport, Iowa, where the boats tied up for the winter. Davenport was the home town of a young boy named Bix Beiderbecke. He was anxious to meet Louis, but Louis never heard Bix play until he got his record, *Singing the Blues*. In Chicago, when Louis played at the Sunset Cafe, Bix made a beeline for the club when he finished his own gig with Paul Whiteman at the Chicago Theatre. After the doors closed at the Sunset, the musicians sat around and jammed.

There were frequent fights on the excursion steamers, and almost everyone working on the boat jumped in to break them up—everyone except the band. They were not allowed to mingle with the whites under any circumstances.

Captain Joe held five dollars a week back from the band members, and gave it all to them when the season ended in Davenport. He also paid their trainfare back to New Orleans. Louis earned more money than he had in his life, and spent it just as fast. He gambled, usually losing, and spent most of what was left on dime store junk for the kids back home. He didn't have to send money home at the time, because both Mayann and Daisy had good jobs of their own.

It was on that first long trip that Louis saw what money could mean to someone, and what it could not. David Jones scrimped and saved every nickel, sending it back home to where some relatives were working a cotton farm for him. Then one day he got word that the farm had been lost. His relatives had been stealing him blind.

Louis worried that Jones might try to kill himself in his depression; but nothing happened. Yet it was a long time before Jones stopped kicking himself for having lost all of his money.

Louis never envied the man who had thirty or forty suits hanging in the closet, or several motor cars in his garage. He figured a man could wear just one suit at a time and drive just one car at a time. He gave away his money whenever he saw someone in need. Years later, Joe Glaser told Tyree Glenn, who was Louis' musical director during the last nine years of his life:

"Pops actually gives away—I mean *gives* away—$500 to $1,000 every damn week. I don't mean every month, I mean every damn *week*."

Time and again Glenn himself saw Louis give his trumpet to a musician who couldn't afford an instrument of his own. When Louis returned to New Orleans after that first six months on the river, his pockets were heavy with cash. He headed for his old stomping grounds at Liberty and Perdido, and the first person he met was Black Benny, standing at the bar in Joe Segretta's saloon.

Benny knew that Louis had been working for Fate Marable, and insisted Louis stand a round of drinks. When he threw a twenty-dollar bill on the bar to pay for the round, Benny scooped up the change and pocketed it.

This hurt. Louis was fond of Black Benny, and if Benny hadn't strong-armed him, probably would have given him much more. He cut out from the saloon as soon as he could, heading for home, where Daisy was waiting with a big pot of red beans and rice.

The reunion was a happy one. Unfortunately, Daisy was Daisy; Louis knew it was only a matter of time before he reverted to her old self.

From time to time Louis tried his hand at songwriting. One composition was called *Get Off Katie's Head;* he sold it to A.J. Piron and Clarence Williams, for a promised $50. They added lyrics and changed the title to *I Wish I Could Shimmy Like My Sister Kate.*

Louis had no contract with Piron and Williams, and they didn't bother putting his name on the music. Nor did he ever get his $50. He accepted the loss philosophically. No one gets everything that's due him in this life.

He stayed with the river boats for three years, taking whatever odd jobs came along during the off season. In 1921, Louis' last year on the steamers, he also worked at Tom Anderson's cabaret on Rampart Street. In the old days Anderson had been king of Storyville, and was still politically strong.

The leader of the four-piece combination at Anderson's was Paul Dominguez, a Creole. Albert Frances played the drums and his wife, Edna, the piano. Later, Wilhelmina Bert Wynn replaced Edna when the latter became pregnant. Louis always felt that they were among the finest piano players he had ever heard, although he later added Lil Hardin to that same exclusive roster.

There was a big kitty in front of the bandstand at Anderson's, and the musicians usually made more in tips than they did in salary. When Anderson closed his cabaret for remodeling, Louis was hired by Zutty Singleton and moved over to Butsy Fernandez's, another cabaret. The piano player there was Udell Wilson, and the trio soon proved popular. Other musicians flocked to see them.

1921 was a slow year, for the national economy and for Louis personally. Business fell off for Butsy, and it was soon an old familiar song: no business, no pay.

The trio stood several salary cuts and then left. Louis still made out better than most, playing parades, funerals and picnics. Toward the end of the year he became a permanent member of the Tuxedo Brass Band. His membership in that organization put him in contact with the finest musicians in the city.

In the same year Daisy adopted a little girl, Wila Mae Wilson. At the time they were living in a white neighborhood at St. Charles and Clio Street, but soon moved to the rear of a white family's home where Daisy was then working. After Louis was mistaken for a burglar while coming home at four in the morning, Daisy gave her notice and they found three rooms at Saratoga and Erato.

Wila Mae was thirteen. Her mother had brought her from a small town in Louisiana, along with her sister, Violet. Violet died at fourteen. Wila Mae continued to live with Daisy after Louis went north to Chicago, until she finally married.

However much Daisy might fight with Louis, while they stayed together she was faithful to him. They did love each other, despite the constant battles. Fighting was in Daisy's blood; she couldn't help herself, help being suspicious of everything Louis did.

After he went north, however, she began to roam. Mama Lucy had gone back to the sawmill town in Florida, where she and her common-law husband prospered, running a small gambling joint.

Life was good, and Louis was happy. In 1922, the

summons came that he'd said would be the only one to take him away. The musicians tried to talk him out of going north to join Oliver, warning him that Oliver had been placed on the musician's union unfair list. At the time there was no union for musicians in New Orleans, so Louis didn't really understand what that meant. All that mattered was that Papa Joe had sent for him.

He wired his acceptance. His last gig in New Orleans was playing for a funeral in Algiers, across the river; the date was August 8, 1922.

The funeral was over, Louis rushed home and threw his few belongings together, then hurried to the Illinois Central Station to catch the train for Chicago. The whole band came to see him off, wishing him luck. They were sorry to see him leaving to take a second cornet position, because they felt Louis was good enough to go out on his own.

It seemed as though the whole neighborhood had turned out at the station. When Louis finally got on the train, even the pullman porters and the waiters recognized him from seeing him playing on the advertising wagons.

"Where are you goin', Dipper?" they asked. "You're a luck sommitch," said one, "to be going North to play with ol' Cocky."

Cocky was a nickname Oliver hated because it referred to one eye, which was badly cataracted. There were some who would never forget it.

The conductor called, "All aboard!"

The train began to move.

Behind him was Louis' youth, and Daisy. The marriage was finished. In his wildest dreams, he could never have imagined what lay before him.

7
CHICAGO!

7

Chicago!

Louis departed the city of New Orleans in the month of August wearing, at Mayann's insistence, his long underwear. Perhaps she had heard stories of the harsh Northern winters. In any event, she feared he would catch a cold before he reached his destination.

On the train, Louis found an empty seat beside a woman and her three children. He had a trout sandwich with him because blacks weren't allowed to eat in the dining cars in the South, which they called Gallilee. The woman had a big basket of fried chicken, enough to last her and her family to California, if they were going that far.

Louis eyed the chicken, wondering how he could cut himself in on the bounty; but before he could ask, the woman recognized him. It turned out she knew Mayann; she was one of the vast numbers of blacks who left the South during the first quarter of this century, to flood into the Northern cities in search of a promised better life. Many of them soon regretted the change, found they had swapped one ghetto for another, this time with Northern winters to chill the blood and an unfamiliar style of life to make them wish they were back home with friends and family.

But many adjusted; and many found themselves better off. For Louis, the long train journey was made easier, at least, by a friendly face to share the hours. As the train drew nearer to Chicago, however, he wondered if anyone would be there to meet him. Joe Oliver had expected him on the early morning train, but Louis had taken the funeral as a last chance to put a little extra money in his pocket.

His fears were realized when the train pulled into the old LaSalle Street Station. There was no familiar face on the platform, nor in the waiting room above. It was 11:30 at night, and the women and the other blacks who had come on the train were getting into taxis or meeting relatives who were waiting for them. The chicken lady and her children said good-bye, and a few minutes later Louis was alone in front of the station.

Louis gave three different versions of what happened next, in *Swing That Music, My Life in New Orleans*, and the Richard Meryman interview. Robert Goffin gave a fourth in *Horn of Plenty*, that most fanciful of all.

In *Swing That Music*, Louis said simply that he went straight to the Lincoln Gardens upon his arrival. It was a big place, with a balcony all around the dance floor, and he felt a little frightened, wondering how he would fit in. Then the boys in the band, most of whom were from New Orleans, greeted him, and everything was all right.

In *My Life in New Orleans*, he said that after he had been standing by himself for half an hour, a policeman came over to ask if he were looking for someone. Louis explained that he had come from New Orleans to join Joe Oliver's jazz band.

"Oh," said the cop, "you're the young man who's to join King Oliver's band at the Lincoln Gardens."

Does anyone really talk like that? It would be interesting to find Louis' original manuscript of his two books for comparison's sake. In any event, a minute passed before it struck Louis that the cop had said *King* Oliver. While he had been king in New Orleans, his name had been just plain Joe.

The cop then told Louis that Joe Oliver had been there earlier, but had to go to the Gardens to play. He'd left word for the policeman to look out for Louis. The cop summoned a cab and told the driver to take Louis to the Lincoln Gardens.

In the Meryman interview, the cop had become a red cap, who guided Louis to the Gardens himself. But according to Goffin, a frightened Louis finally asked a bootblack for directions, to be told that the man had never heard of the Lincoln Gardens. When the bootblack saw that Louis was near panic he took pity on him, and told him to look up the address in the phone book. Even here, according to Goffin, Louis had trouble, the implication being that he didn't know how to use a telephone directory.

A kindly white samaritan finally helped him, and told him where to take the El to the south side. His adventures finding his way about a strange city late at night were harrowing, but such flights of fancy are to be found time and time again in Goffin's book. It's a shame that Goffin can't be counted on more, but since so many of his events fail to tally with other published versions, the book takes on the ring of fantasy. Further, in his attempts to describe a strange and foreign milieu to his readers, who were, after all, Europeans, Goffin seems to have accepted at face value all of the wilder tales of America of that time.

Goffin went on to say that when Louis finally reached the Lincoln Gardens, he was nearly turned away by a uniformed doorman, who assumed he was looking for kitchen work. Louis did have the appearance of a bumpkin when he first arrived in Chicago. Max Jones reported that Preston Jackson, who knew Dippermouth from their school days—apparently shared—was struck by his country-boy appearance that night:

"He wore a brown box-back coat, straw hat and tan shoes." But he "played a horn like nobody had ever heard."

As Louis opened the big doors to the Lincoln Gardens, he heard Joe Oliver's band swinging one of the good old Dixieland tunes. He wondered if he could ever hold his own with such a fine group of musicians.

The Gardens was located at 31st and Cottage Grove Avenues, a building recently remodeled. It had a beautiful front and a canopy that crossed the sidewalk. Perhaps there was a doorman. Max Jones said that the Gardens, when packed, could hold a thousand paying customers.

There was also a cabaret, featuring such well-known performers and singers of the day as Ethel Waters. Revues were held in the cabaret, with half a dozen acts. The entire show might run to sixty musicians and performers.

Louis remembered later that the lobby that night seemed a block long. The place was jammed with customers, for Joe Oliver's Creole Jazz Band was one of the most popular dance bands in the city. Even the other musicians, who were supposedly upset with Oliver for his union practices, flocked to see him and listen to his jazz.

None of the band members noticed Louis until he was almost to the bandstand; then they jumped up and began to greet him. Oliver chewed tobacco constantly, and had a private cuspidor on which he beat out, with his left foot, the tempo of the piece they were to play. He took his foot off the cuspidor and demanded that Louis tell everything that had happened to him and the folks in New Orleans during the past four years.

When the break finished, the band returned to playing while Louis sat down in a corner to listen to the music for the rest of the night. When at last the show finished, Joe Oliver took Louis to his own house around the corner, where Stella Oliver was as glad to see him as was her husband.

Living with the Olivers was Stella's daughter by another marriage, Ruby. Louis felt that they were a happy family, Joe then on top of the world. They made him welcome with open arms, and even though it was late, Stella made him sit down and fed both Louis and Joe red beans and rice. There was also a half loaf of bread and a bucket of ice-cold lemonade. Lemonade and sugar water were the beverages Joe liked best, and Louis took many of his meals with the Olivers. Both were expert trenchermen, and Stella was fond of feeding them.

Then Joe summoned a cab and took Louis to the boarding house where he had reserved a room for him on South Wabash Avenue. The boarding house was run by a Creole woman named Filo, who had left New Orleans ten years earlier.

Joe told Louis during the cab ride that he had a room with a private bath, which Louis greeted with a certain amount of disbelief. Back in New Orleans the black people had never heard of such a thing as a bathtub, much less a private bath. When he lived with Mayann, a privy in the backyard served all of the little houses around it. It was emptied once a week.

The residents of Louis' neighborhood took their baths in a washtub in the backyard, or in a tin foot tub. In the foot tub, it was necessary to sit on the rim and wash from neck to middle, and then stand and wash the rest.

Filo was an attractive middle-aged woman, as lonely as most for news of home. She had been waiting for them to arrive, and Louis immediately felt at home. He was anxious to see his private bath, but for a time he had to sit and talk about New Orleans.

The next day he slept late, then spent the afternoon roaming the city and taking in the sights. By now he was used to skyscrapers and the like from visiting St. Louis on the excursion steamers, but it was still more than he could take in all at once.

There are several versions of when he started to play with the band. In *Swing That Music*, Louis himself said that he needed a certain amount of rehearsal and did not sit in for the first time until the next week. Other versions had him starting the second night. According to Goffin, he sat in the night he arrived.

The first night he did play, he dressed in what Louis called his old Roast Beef, which was his nickname for his raggedy tuxedo. It was patched here and there, but neatly pressed. The first people he met when he arrived at the Lincoln Gardens were Mrs. Major, the white owner of the club, and Red Bud, the black manager. King Jones, a short man with a loud voice, was the M.C. Louis implied that Jones tried to pass for white but fooled no one.

The audience began to fill the hall while the band had a last smoke before beginning its first set. Out front were some of the finest musicians in town, including bandleader Isham Jones and Louis Panico, his white trumpeter. Louis was still unknown, but word had spread through town that a new young cornet player had come north to join Joe Oliver.

In the Oliver band were Johnny and Baby Dodds, Honore Dutrey, Bill Johnson, a piano player, and a second cornet which Louis had come to replace, and the King. In *My Life in New Orleans* and other late-life reminiscences, Louis said Lil Hardin was the piano player, but Max Jones said that his memory had failed him. Louis frequently telescoped several events of those days together.

Lil Hardin Armstrong herself said:

"Late in May, 1921, King Oliver's band went to San Francisco, Cal., to play a six-months engagement at the Pergola Ballroom (949 Market Street.) When the job closed I returned to Chicago, but the rest of the band stayed out there an additional six months. Oliver brought Bertha Gonzales back to Chicago in 1922 and it was then that Louis joined him at the Royal Gardens. Some months later Bertha left and I went back with the band."

While the Oliver band was away from Chicago for a year the Royal Gardens was remodeled and renamed the Lincoln Gardens. Max Jones said that Bertha Gonzales was usually called "Gonsoulin" in those days. She was supposed to have developed her style from that of Jelly Roll Morton. Louis never mentioned her in any of his books or reminiscences, so it has been assumed that she was not particularly memorable as a performer. Lil Hardin said she never heard Bertha play because they worked the same hours. Bertha dropped from sight for twenty years, then in 1943 made a brief reappearance as Bertha "Gonzolon" with the suddenly rediscovered Bunk Johnson.

Before the trip to San Francisco, Lil Hardin played with the Oliver band at the Dreamland and the Pekin Cafes; the latter was a favored hangout for the mobsters of the time. Louis was aware of Lil before he traveled north, because Joe had sent a picture of his band to New Orleans the year before.

In *Swing That Music*, Louis said: ". . . and the pianst in the band was an attractive looking brown-skinned girl named Lillian Hardin. I had said in my next letter to [Joe], 'Tell Miss Lil I like her.' "

One night, soon after he joined the Oliver band, Joe took Louis to the Dreamland, to meet Lil for the first time. It was two or three months after that before she rejoined the band at the Lincoln Gardens.

Lil herself remembered: "Finally, while I was working at the Dreamland, Joe brought Louis over to meet me. I'd been hearing from all the musicians about him—Little Louis, they'd called him—and what a good player he was. So they brought him in and 'Li'l Louis' was all of 226 pounds."

In a TV interview many years later, Lil expanded on Louis' size: " 'How come you call him 'Li'l Louis,' as big as he is?' I asked the other musicians. 'Well, he's been following us around since he was a little boy,' they replied.' "

She added, "I wasn't impressed at all, I was very disappointed. 226 pounds. I didn't like anything about him. I didn't like the way he was dressed; I was very disgusted. So he came on the bandstand—I don't know if I should tell this or not—and I used to, you know . . . girls wore garters on their stockings, so when I'd sit down to play I would roll my stocking down so the garter was below my knee, for circulation. And the first thing Louis spied was my knee. And he was looking, and I said, 'This guy's got ideas he'd better not put into words.' "

After Joe Oliver's aid to the young Louis in New Orleans, Lil Hardin was to prove perhaps the most important influence of his life. She was a graduate of Fisk University and a conservatory-trained classical pianist. Valedictorian of her class at Fisk, Lil came from Memphis but moved to Chicago with her family in 1917. Apparently one of her first jobs was at the Dreamland, where she was introduced to jazz by Delta bandsmen.

Lil's exact age is uncertain. At the time of Louis' death, she was said to be someplace between sixty-seven and seventy. She may have been older than Louis.

Louis reported in *Swing That Music* that Lil continued her studies even after they married. They practiced together, sometimes playing classical music. He had learned to transpose from a piano part, and working with Lil sharpened his reading ability.

From the first, Lil apparently felt that Louis should not have been playing a second cornet position to Joe Oliver. Once she got over her earlier, obviously unwarranted dislike of him, she began to push him toward greater things.

With Louis, Joe Oliver presented a kind of music

never before heard, or attempted. The two-cornet breaks were something new. Louis said:

"They didn't understand how we did it, without music or anything. I had second trumpet notes for all them riffs and breaks we made. So many you hear today were originated by Joe Oliver, and I had notes for every one of them. Couldn't nobody trick us; the musicians thought we were marvellous."

Clarinettist Buster Bailey explained the secret of their technique; "What Joe was going to make in the middle break, he'd make in the first ending. Louis would listen and remember; then when the middle came, Oliver and Louis would both take that same break together."

Whatever the technique, together, Joe Oliver and Louis made musical history. But after Louis had been with the band a while, he looked up from the bandstand one night to see Mayann plowing through the crowd, two big paper-wrapped bundles under her arm and her face set and determined.

Someone had told her that Louis was doing very badly in Chicago, was even thinking about suicide. Upon hearing that news, she had packed her things and caught the next train north.

There was a happy reunion, and Mayann sat on the bandstand the rest of the night; Joe Oliver dedicated a number to her. Her original intention had been to turn around and head back to New Orleans once she was sure that things were all right with her son; but Louis talked her into staying. He rented her an apartment and bought her new clothes; but after awhile Mayann got homesick for her friends and her church. She said she had to go back to New Orleans and show off all of her finery.

Several years later, after Louis and Lil had married

and bought a house together, Mayann became seriously ill. Lil went to New Orleans and brought her back to Chicago. By then Louis had made his first trip to New York, to play with Fletcher Henderson's orchestra. He was away from Chicago a year.

Speaking of that second of Mayann's visits north, Lil said: "She died in this house on East 44th Street I'm still living in—the house Louis and I purchased in 1925."

In the Meryman interview, Louis said, "I used to take Mama cabareting, and we'd get soused together. Used to have a very nice time. Yeah, I miss old Mayann. Her funeral in Chicago is probably the only time I ever cried—when they put the cover over her face.

"I was making money and she had a beautiful funeral. Thank God for that. Didn't have to put the saucer on her. I've seen that happen to many of 'em—don't have no insurance or belong to no club. While you laying out there in the wake, they put a saucer on your chest and everybody who comes in drops a nickel or a dime or quarter to try to make up for the undertaker."

Mayann was in her early forties when she died. She had married Willie Armstrong at fifteen, although the exact age at which she had given birth to Louis is uncertain. She wanted to be buried in New Orleans, but the funeral was in Chicago. The loss of his mother struck Louis hard.

Lil Hadin's interest in Louis was finally given life by a remark made by Joe Oliver: "One night he told me: 'You know this Louis, he's a better trumpet player than I'll ever be . . . As long as I keep him playing second to me he won't get ahead of me. I'll still be the king.' "

Early in 1923 the Creole Jazz Band went on tour through Illinois, Ohio and Indiana. They stopped in Richmond, Indiana, and made their first recordings in the studios of the Starr Piano Company. The date has variously been given as March 31 and April 6. Nine sides were cut for the company's Gennett label: *Just Gone, Canal Street Blues, Mandy Lee Blues, I'm Going Away to Wear You Off My Mind, Chimes Blues, Weather Bird Rag, Dippermouth Blues, Froggie Moore* and *Snake Rag*.

Three of the numbers were originals by Joe Oliver. The band was nervous in the unfamiliar surroundings. The only person said to be at ease was Lil Hardin. There were no drums at the session; the acoustic recording equipment of the day couldn't handle them. A drum roll made the recording needle jump right off the track.

This was also before the day of the microphone. The band played into a large horn, essentially a megaphone on a stand. The one pick-up had to suffice for all of the instruments. It took some time to find the proper balance, because when Louis and Joe stood next to each other, as they did on the bandstand, Louis' volume drowned out all of the other instruments. At last they had to place him in the corner, fifteen or twenty feet away.

Louis was unhappy with the arrangement, but Lil reassured him that it was all right. As for herself, she was at last convinced that if Louis had to be put that far away from the others, then he had to be better than Joe Oliver.

Joe, Louis later remembered, was already past his prime at thirty-eight. Perhaps what he had said to Lil was merely a recognition that he could no longer compete with his protege. Later, Louis frequently commented that it was a shame no recordings were made of the music that was heard in New Orleans during the first decade of the century. Some of the greatest performances and performers of all time were thus lost to posterity.

Later that year the band cut further sides for Gennett, OKeh, Columbia and Paramount. During 1923, Louis contacted a lawyer, who arranged his divorce from Daisy. He married Lil Hardin on February 5, 1923.

Lil kept pushing Louis to better himself, and finally Ollie Powers offered him a first trumpet spot at the Dreamland. Perhaps because of Lil's influence, Louis realized there was no future for him with Joe Oliver. The Creole Jazz Band had room for just one lead cornet, and that horn was Papa Joe.

Robert Goffin said that when the band went on tour the first time, many of the musicians were reluctant to leave Chicago. They tried to talk Joe into canceling the tour, but he had already signed the contracts. Goffin said that Joe, worried, discussed the situation with Louis, who suggested that he replace the dropouts with a new group of musicians who had just come up from New Orleans.

In that way, Honore Dutrey, the Dodds brothers and Bill Johnson left the Oliver band, to be replaced by Buster Bailey on the clarinet, Johnny Lindsay on bass fiddle, Rudy Jackson, saxophone, and Buddy Christian on the banjo.

The band returned to Lincoln Gardens after the tour, but left again soon after Louis married Lil to tour through Ohio, Wisconsin, Michigan and Pennsylvania. It was back to Chicago in May, and Louis left the organization in early June, for a short layoff, then joined Powell at the Dreamland. Oliver's tour resumed through Illinois, Indiana and Pennsylvania.

''Apparently the Lincoln Gardens were shuttered during at least part of these tours. Again according to Goffin, the streak of bad luck that began for Joe Oliver with Louis' departure continued: that summer the Lincoln Gardens was destroyed by fire. When he returned to Chicago, he found a place as soloist in Dave Payton's band at the Plantation Band, but taking a step down hurt. He tried to get Louis to join him in a new combo that would replace Payton, but it was too late.

Louis had received Fletcher Henderson's second invitation to come to New York. This time he accepted.

8
NEW YORK, NEW YORK; AND CHICAGO AGAIN . . .

8

New York, New York; and Chicago again . . .

Fletcher Henderson's band played at Roseland, the famous New York City dance hall which is still in business at Broadway and 51st Street. Lil traveled to New York with Louis, although she had to return to Chicago after two weeks because her mother was seriously ill.

Robert Goffin would have us believe that on the day they arrived, Louis left Lil in Grand Central Station to guard the luggage while he spent the rest of the day taking in the sights of the city. Considering Lil's reputation as a strong-willed woman, this seems an unlikely version of the events of the day. When he returned to Chicago a year later, some of the other musicians kidded Louis because in his home life he always seemed to defer to Lil. She ordered his actions, his dress, and, it was said, everything else, until even Louis became embarrassed by the measure of control he had given up.

Some of the musicians nicknamed him "Hennie"—short for henpecked. Louis himself wrote later:

"The guys who called me Henpeck all the time were broke all the time. And I always had a pocket full of money. Lots of outside people tried to interfere with Lil and my marriage . . . We were both young, and Lil with the better education and experience only did what any wife would do. Everything she bought for me were the best, clothes—the very best, and her suggestions were all perfect. I appreciate them all."

Lil came back to New York several times during the next year, but never for more than a few days at a time. Perhaps the long separation was a mistake, although Louis wrote her a letter every day they were apart. He had taken quarters in Harlem, where a few people knew who he was. Downtown, he felt completely lost in the nation's largest city.

The Henderson band was not noted for its jazz, but it was by far the most famous black band in the country. It has been reported that Louis was offered $55 a week to join Henderson, certainly less than Joe Oliver had been paying him. Louis said that Oliver paid him $52 a week when he first came north from New Orleans; Robert Goffin reported the figure was $30 a week. Whichever is correct, it was far more than he had made in New Orleans.

When Louis left Joe Oliver in May, 1924, Lil apparently stayed with the Oliver band for a while. She told Joe, diplomatically, that Louis would soon be back; but to herself she thought that such a thing would happen only over her dead body.

Roseland always had two bands booked at the same time. Sam Lanin led the other when Louis joined Henderson. Louis said Henderson had twelve pieces at the time, but apparently there were only nine when he joined the organization: the standard two saxes, two trumpets, one trombone, banjo, piano, drums and tuba. Henderson wanted to go to a third trumpet; in fact, he had been doing just that on some of his records, with Joe Smith filling the third chair.

At the same time that Louis joined the band, Buster Bailey was hired on his recommendation, which raised the number of pieces to eleven. Louis' joining the Henderson orchestra was as exciting to other musicians in town as it had been in Chicago, although his presence meant little to the general public. Don Redmond claimed that the Henderson's band concept of music changed radically with Louis' arrival. The differences can be heard by comparing pre-Louis and post-Louis records. It has also been said that much of the Henderson's recordings were undistinguished, except for Louis' sometimes-shattering solos.

Kaiser Marshall, Henderson's drummer, was quoted by Max Jones on the first meeting of the band with Satch:

"I remember the day that Louis showed up for rehearsal. We were up at the Happy Rhone Club at 143rd Street and Lennox Avenue that we used for rehearsals. The band was up and on the stand waiting when he got there, and Louis walked across the floor. He had on big thick-soled shoes, the kind policemen wear, and he came walking across the floor, clump-clump, and grinned and said hello to all the boys."

Marshall continued: "He got his seat and opened the book for the third trumpet. Now Fletcher Henderson's book wasn't one that just anybody could open up and read at sight. He had a lot of difficult arrangements there . . . and although Louis was a good reader at that time, he had a little trouble at first. He would make a mistake, and jump up and say: 'Man, what is that thing?' Then everybody laughed and Louis would sit down and play it right the next time. After he made one mistake he didn't make it again. We got along fine . . ."

Fletcher Henderson remembered that the arrangement was a new one of beautiful Irish waltzes. That was not quite what Louis was used to. Faced with the strange material, he tried his best to make everyone laugh to dissolve the tension.

Rex Stewart, the cornetist, was also quoted by Jones: ". . . Louis hit town. I went mad . . . I tried to walk like him, talk like him, eat like him, sleep like him. Finally I got to shake hands and talk with him."

The Henderson musicians kidded Louis about his shoes and about his long underwear until at last he took them off. The band played many record dates, for which they received bonuses; and sometimes when Roseland closed, traveled to Harlem to play an extra hour. Each man received $25 for that one hour of play.

Most of them were living high, enjoying the money while they had it. They bought English walking suits at $110 when a common laborer might buy a tailor-made for $10 off the rack. They also wore $7 spats and $18 shoes. According to Kaiser Marshall, Louis saved his money.

Louis cut more than forty sides with Fletcher Henderson, in most of which only his playing lifts the cuts about the mediocre. He also cut many dates on the sides with top blues singers such as Bessie Smith, Ma Rainey, Maggie Jones, Chippie Hill, Clara Smith, Trixie Smith, Alberta Hunter and Virginia Liston.

Bessie Smith was almost unfriendly, perhaps resenting sharing the limelight with Louis, who was only a backup man on her recordings. Smith was a quiet woman, but with a quick temper. She was already a legend, and one day someone decided to test her reputation as a walking bank. He asked for change for a thousand dollar bill. Bessie raised up the front of her dress, revealing a carpenter's apron, and counted out the change.

Louis also cut several sides with Clarence Williams' Blue Five, which was the free-wheeling type of jazz group he preferred. Later, on one or more of Lil's visits, he cut a series with a group known as the Red Onion Jazz Babies. Lil played the piano on these, and Sidney Bechet joined him on several of the Blue Five and Red Onion sessions. Others on the Red Onion cuttings were Buster Bailey, Buddy Christian and Charlie Irvis.

Louis lamented later that Henderson would not let him sing with his orchestra, thus losing the experience he had gained in Chicago. But Lil Armstrong claimed later that she didn't remember him singing with the Oliver band; nor are there any vocals on the records cut with Oliver. In fact, his first recorded vocal was breaks that Louis sang on the take of Fletcher Henderson's *Everybody Loves My Baby*.

Thursday night was vaudeville night at Roseland, with a talent competition. Louis played and sang the same number, winning first prize. After that, his performances became a favorite with the Thursday night crowds. Perhaps he was bitter because he was never allowed to record his show version of the tune.

With Fletcher Henderson, Louis appeared at the Apollo Theatre in Harlem, the Roxy in Manhattan, and other famous places of the day. Shortly after he arrived Louis bought a new tuxedo, paying $50. He was proud of the outfit, and delighted in dressing up in the stiff-bosomed shirt. There might have been some reluctance at joining the Henderson band, because he had to take the third chair. He had been second to Fate Marable and to Joe Oliver.

Louis was popular in Harlem, where he was known from his records with the Creole Jazz Band. He was particularly proud to be asked to do a trumpet solo at the Savoy Dance Hall in Harlem, where his success prompted a repeat invitation. However, on Broadway he was just another musician in the Henderson ensemble, so far as the paying public was concerned. Five years were to pass before New York welcomed him to its heart.

Robert Goffin says that while Lil was absent in Chicago, Louis met a dancer named Fanny, a chorus girl at the Cotton Club in Harlem. She was pretty and witty, a marvelous singer and an excellent dancer. Louis fell, hard. In April, 1925, Henderson took his band on a road trip through New England and Pennsylvania, playing one night stands. The orchestra was frequently in competition with the best white bands appearing at other clubs, but Henderson scored well in popularity.

While they were in Boston, Fanny appeared in the audience. The relationship was renewed for the night, but she had to leave the next day. Goffin says that in a rash moment, Louis promised to marry her. When the orchestra returned to New York, he spent the day looking for her all over town; but Fanny had gone to Pennsylvania.

That night he received a letter from Lil: an ultimatum to return to Chicago or forget the marriage. It must be assumed that Louis' guilty conscience made him go to Henderson to and tell him that the time had come to return to Chicago. She had taken a job with Bill Bottoms' Dreamland—which was not the Dreamland Ballroom, mentioned earlier. She told Louis in her letter that she had a featured spot for him at $75 a week.

Whether or not the story of Fanny is true is uncertain, although Goffin said she made a later appearance in Chicago that proved equally uncomfortable to Louis. It is apparent that he was unhappy with the situation in the Henderson orchestra. The other musicians drank heavily, would come on the bandstand unable even to keep time. In 1945 he told Barry Ulanov:

"When them cats commenced getting careless with their music, fooling around all night, I was dragged, man."

Twenty-one years later he repeated the complaint to Richard Meryman. Fletcher Henderson, however, said that Louis left because he wanted to form his own band. This may have been the excuse given. Certainly Henderson was never bitter, because there were future offers for Louis to rejoin his organization.

Probably the pressure from Lil was the little bit extra that Louis needed to send him back to Chicago. The experience of working in New York had been tremendously worthwhile, however, for him professionally. Max Jones said that in that year Louis gained confidence, improved his knowledge of reading music and interpreting a score, learned many new tricks of showmanship and picked up ideas from dozens of the musicians he heard perform.

Louis returned to Chicago in early November to join Lil Armstrong's Dreamland Syncopators. A short time later he cut the first of the Hot 5 sides of OKeh Records, with Johnny Dodds on clarinet, Kid Ory on trombone, Johnny St. Cyr on banjo and guitar, and Lil on piano.

This was strictly a pick-up group which never played together outside of a recording studio.

Collectors pay a great deal of money for the original pressings of the early Armstrong groups. The most desirable of all are those he made with the Creole Jazz Band on the Gennett label. According to Rare Records, of Glendale, California, pressings in very good condition of the Oliver sides are worth from $100 to $200.

The Fletcher Henderson recordings are not as valuable because the cuts themselves are generally undistinguished, except for Louis' playing. However, the sides cut with the Blue Five and the Red Onion Jazz Babies bring from $50 to $100. The Hot 5's are a $25-$50 item, while the Hot 7's, made a little later, are worth a little less. Louis made one famous recording on his first trip to Hollywood in 1930, backing up Jimmie Rodgers on *Blue Yodel #9*. A Rodgers item is considered worth $25-$30, for very few Armstrong collectors seek this particular cut.

Many of these early recordings are still available today for those interested in the early Armstrong but not in paying collector's prices, re-released on long-playing albums.

Louis was physically small, but broad-shouldered and shortnecked; when he blew his horn, his neck swelled until it was almost as large as his head. Despite his weight, he had a light walk that belied his massive frame.

In December, he was asked to join Erskine Tate's fifteen-piece pit orchestra at the Vendome Theater. The pit band played the scores for the silent movies and an overture when the curtain rose at the beginning of the program. Some of the musicians did a solo on stage; Louis' favorite number was the classical *Cavalleria*

Rusticana.

Erskine's brother, Jimmy, played trumpet in the orchestra, and it was thought it would be best if Louis did the same. So he switched. Three great jazz pianists followed one another into the Erskine orchestra: Teddy Weatherford, Earl Hines and Fats Waller. Louis played an occasional trumpet and organ duet with Fats.

At the Vendome he also had a solo specialty of *Heebie Jeebies,* during which he sang two choruses: the first straight, and the second with nonsense "scat" syllables. He recorded the same routine, and the scat chorus became so well-known that it was reprinted on the piano and vocal scores of the song.

Early in 1926 Louis left Lil's band, to join Carroll Dickerson at the Sunset, on April 10. The Sunset was owned by Joe Glaser, the first time Louis met the man who would be his manager for most of his professional career. That was a few years later, however.

It has been suggested that this was when Louis first started seeing Alpha Smith, a girl of fifteen or sixteen who worked as a maid for a white family. Apparently the domestic situation was anything but smooth at the time, and there had been a number of separations.

"Whenever we'd break up," said Louis, "we'd draw all of our money out of the bank and split it up."

Matters were further complicated by the presence of Clarence. Louis had brought the boy to Chicago in 1925, moving him first into an apartment and then into the house he bought with Lil. According to Robert Goffin, Louis had already spoken to a lawyer about a divorce; Lil and her mother took things out on Clarence.

Goffin said that Alpha came out of the audience one night at the Vendome, after the show, and impulsively

kissed Louis. When he got home, Lil wanted to know
who left the lipstick on him. After that, Alpha came to
the Vendome for the twice-weekly change in shows.
Louis began seeing her on the side, calling at Alpha's
mother's house almost every evening. One day he took
Clarence along, and they feasted on fried chicken and
red beans. Clarence would have been nine or ten at the
time; he supposedly told Louis that night that he wanted
to leave Lil and move in with Alpha.

Shortly after Louis went to work at the Sunset, he
came to work one night to see his name up in lights:
Louis Armstrong, World's Greatest Trumpeter!

Early in 1927 Glaser made Louis the leader of the
band. That was a position Louis never liked to take, for
he wanted to have none of the responsibilities that came
with leadership. Details of running the operation were
an annoyance that kept him from playing his music.

He made Earl Hines musical director of the band,
which was now called Louis Armstrong and His
Stompers. Louis continued to double with Erskine Tate
at the Vendome until April, when he left and moved
over to double with Clarence Jones' Orchestra at the
Metropolitan Theatre.

Some of the record would indicate that Louis worked
almost constantly, but he was no more than human.
From time to time he lost days and even weeks to illness.
December, 1926 was lost in that way.

In the Sunset band, under his name, there were such
men as Earl Hines and Buck Washington on piano,
Tubby Hall on Drums, Peter Briggs, tuba, Honore Dutrey, trombone, Rip Basset, Joe Dixon and Al Washington, saxes, and Boyd Atkins on banjo. He loved his
music so much that after finishing at the Sunset, he frequently went to other clubs for long jam sessions. De-

spite the domestic problems, from 1925 through 1928, Louis and Lil together made good money. Besides the house, they bought a car and some lots on Lake Idlewild that helped support Lil Armstrong in her later years.

Joe Oliver was still playing at the Plantation when Louis moved to the Sunset; the two clubs were across the street from each other. Soon the crowds began moving to the new attraction, switching their allegiance. Louis offered to help Joe in whatever way he could, but Oliver accepted the situation philosophically. He seemed to know that his time had passed, that he had to make room for the younger man.

Lil Armstrong had done much work for the Oliver band, composing and writing new arrangements down on paper. However, she personally felt that Freddie Keppard was superior to Oliver as a player.

Cab Calloway was the intermission at the Sunset at that time. He had come to Chicago to study law, but his sister worked in the show and got him the singing job.

From November 1925 through December 1928, Louis cut more than sixty sides with his own small groups and many more with other ensembles put together by John Dodds, Erskine Tate, Carroll Dickerson, and others. It has been said that Louis revolutionized jazz instrumentals. In the early days of Ma Rainey and Bessie Smith, the instrumental was considered only as support for the singer. Louis liberated the jazz artist from the constraints of the past.

The Hot 7 recordings added Baby Dodds on drums and Pete Briggs on tuba; John Thomas replaced Kid Ory on the trombone. These early records were considered immensely successful when they sold forty thousand copies, although popular white bands and singers of the day, such as Paul Whiteman and Gene Austin, sold in the hundreds of thousands. Austin was the first singer to sell more than a million copies of a single disc.

The musicians on these pickup sessions received no royalties. Each man got $50 a session, and were glad to do it. If they wrote a song, they sold it outright. Louis would write four or five songs at a session, sitting on his front steps, then take them downtown and peddle them for a quick dollar. Sometimes he added lyrics, but these were always reworked. Among the songs he wrote at that time were *Gut Bucket Blues, Drop That Sack, Old Man Mose* and *Struttin' with Some Barbecue*.

Eventually Louis' records were marketed in England and in Europe, where the audience was far more willing to accept jazz than the American public. His later releases were issued in Britain by Parlophone, and were so popular that they stayed in the catalogue nearly thirty years.

At some point along about then, Louis and Lil engaged in a royal battle. The upshot was that Louis and Clarence moved out of the house and in with Alpha's mother. According to Goffin, Louis spent a great deal of money on Alpha, once showed up at her house driving a new Model T with yellow wheels. When the neighbors gathered around, Alpha stepped out, wearing a new powder blue dress. A short time later Louis rented an apartment for Clarence and himself, where Alpha would stop in to see him on her way home from a new job in a downtown department store.

Louis had an exclusive contract with OKeh, and so much of his outside recording was either anonymous or under an assumed name. Lil's Hot Shots was one of those groups, but was really only the Hot 5 renamed. Johnny Dodds had a contract with Vocalion, and once he asked Louis to cut a vocal for him.

The two sides for Johnny were *Wild Man Blues* and *Melancholy*. A few weeks after the record went on sale the president of OKeh asked Louis to come to his office. When Louis came in, the president said nothing but put a record on the phonograph; and when the side finished, asked Louis if he knew the singer's identity.

Louis mumbled his reply: "I dunno; but I won't do it again!"

The later Hot 5 recordings actually had six musicians, an entirely different group, except for Louis. Earl Hines was on the piano, Zutty Singleton, his old friend from New Orleans, on the drums, Fred Robinson, trombone, Jimmy Strong, clarinet and tenor sax, and Mancy Carr on banjo and guitar. After Louis rejoined Carroll Dickerson at the Savoy ballroom, the group was renamed the Savoy Ballroom 5, with Don Redman replacing Strong on clarinet and alto.

While Louis continued at the Sunset, there were outside engagements, including two weeks at the Blackhawk. Cutting contests were popular among jazz musicians, where the challenger tried to prove himself better. One time Freddie Keppard borrowed Louis' trumpet and gave out with some of his finest choruses. When he finished, he looked at Louis without a word, daring him to be better.

Louis took his trumpet, Lil urging him: "Now get him!" She remembered later that Louis had never played better in his life. When he finished, Keppard had disappeared. After that, no one else ever asked for Satch's trumpet.

The challenges continued, however. Hot Lips Page, quoted by Max Jones, remembered one cutting contest:

"I remember I was eating with Pops in a restaurant when I overheard four young cats arranging to cut Pops that evening. Man, it was to be murder; when one guy's lips gave out, the other would take over. Pops never looks up from his fried chicken, but that night he let those cats start and as they played he pulled up a little cafe table and set a chair on it and climbs up and let go. Those four cool guys faded out one after the other, put their horns away and just slunk out.''

Louis remained at the Sunset until the end of 1927, when apparently Earl Hines got into an argument with Joe Glaser. They both quit, and with Zutty Singleton, took a lease on Warwick Hall, intending to open their own club. The band was known as Louis Armstrong's Hot Six. Zutty was perhaps Louis' best friend in those days, and they spent a great deal of time together makng the rounds of the night clubs and cabarets. Louis usually picked up the tab.

According to Robert Goffin, in his innocence Louis singed a lease for a year at a monthly rental of $375. They didn't know that a new dance hall a few blocks away was scheduled to open on the same day. This was the Savoy Ballroom, where Louis took a job the next year. Goffin said the facade of the Savoy sported peacocks that preened themselves in brilliant colors.

Although the trio played out their hearts, the opening was disastrous; almost no one came. They struggled on for a few days, then threw in the towel. Jazz no longer had the popularity of a few years earlier; sweet music was the current rage. Goffin reports that the trio locked the Warwich for the last time and walked off to Louis' car . . . which had been stolen.

This makes a fitting end to a sad story. Unfortunely, there is no corroboration that such an event really happened. A short time later the partners decided to make one more try and found a place on the West Side, taking it just for the night. They put on a dance, but trouble broke out; and in the excitement, the cash drawer vanished. They were out of business for good.

In February, Louis again joined Clarence Jones for a time; and in March he rejoined Carroll Dickerson at the Savoy Ballroom, which had put him out of business. Things began to pick up, for Dickerson broadcast regularly from the Savoy over a national hookup. This brought Louis to the attention of an audience that had not heard him on his records.

Life wasn't all music and domestic problems. There was time for games. While still at the Sunset, the musicians organized a baseball game against the waiters. Louis bought the equipment, and when he got angry, picked everything up and went home.

The Dickerson band accepted a basketball challenge from the Clarence Black orchestra. Louis weighed over 220 at the time, and was unable to find, in all of Chicago, a basketball uniform to fit. At last he turned out for the game wearing his bathing trunks.

"When we went out there, we upset the joint," said Louis. "But the game tore me up. I didn't know it took that much wind to play the game. I was so tired when that ball did get in my hands, and Zutty yelled out 'Dribble it,' well, I put it against my chest and ran to the basket. Then I missed. They told me all of the rules I broke. You shoulda heard them fans howl."

Goffin reports the score was 2 to 0, Louis' team losing. That night Louis was exhausted, but he still managed to play at the Savoy. However, he was out sick with exhaustion for the next week or more.

Louis remained with Dickerson for the rest of 1928, although he took a few outside gigs. In May, he accepted a two-day engagement to front Floyd Campbell's

band on the Streckfus excursion boat *St. Paul*, out of
St. Louis. Louis received $100 a day plus expenses.

However, there was no attempt made to limit the
number of tickets sold. Five thousand people crowded
aboard the steamer, which was dangerously overloaded.
The captain feared that the boat would capsize and returned to St. Louis early, angering the crowd. By so
doing, he narrowly avoided a disaster.

Louis was once again earning good money. The
Savoy management had to give him a raise to stave off a
more tempting offer from Fletcher Henderson. But
things began to change in the first months of 1929. They
accepted more outside dates, including one-nights in
Detroit in January, St. Louis in February, and Detroit
again in March.

In March, Louis was called to New York by promoter
Tommy Rockwell for a two-day guest stint with Luis
Russell's band. In the coming years, Louis worked very
closely with Russell. Apparently the marriage to Lil was
over in everything but name, and he was living full time
with Alpha. However, they did not formally separate
until 1931; and Louis did not divorce Lil until 1938.

While in New York in March, Louis cut a record with
a pickup group that included Kaiser Marshall, Jack Teagarden, Eddie Lang, Happy Cauldwell on tenor sax,
and pianist Joe Sullivan. Eddie Condon was also in the
studio during the session and apparently was responsible for bringing the group together. This was Louis'
first recording with Teagarden, and may have been his
first with a mixed band.

One day, according to Goffin, Fanny showed up in
Chicago, looking for Louis. He found himself in an
embarrassing position, for Alpha was nearby at the
time. Fanny tried again, and at last gave up, signing a

contract to tour the continent. Louis promised her that if he ever went to Europe, it would be to see her.

Business turned worse; apparently the Savoy could not or would not meet the band's payroll. Louis guested with Dave Peyton's orchestra at the Regal Theater for a week, and then in mid-May, the band either quit, or was let go.

Louis had received another summons from Tommy Rockwell, who was with OKeh records. There was nothing at the moment in Chicago, and so he decided to try New York again. Although the summons had been just for him, the Dickerson band talked it over, and decided to go with him.

9
TRAVELIN' JAZZ MAN

9
Travelin' Jazz Man

The reason for the Savoy Ballroom's failure is unknown, although forty years later Max Jones speculated that competition from a new and luxurious Grand Terrace, where the band was led by Earl Hines, coupled with the arrival of "talkies," were at least part of the story. Al Capone was a frequent visitor to the Grand Terrace, which obviously had connections to the mob. Hites remembered that Capone would order the doors to the club closed for himself and his henchmen; the band was told to play his favorite numbers. Capone was liberal with $100 tips.

Louis had his own troubles with the mob over the years, although even late in his life he refused to elaborate. He once changed managers when he was threatened with violence, and hired two bodyguards who stayed with him for months. But that came later, before his triumphant return to New Orleans in 1931.

Tommy Rockwell had summoned Louis for a Vincent Youmans show called "Horseshoes." The title was later changed to "Great Day," or so Louis remembered it. Carroll Dickerson was still leader of the band, but everyone agreed that Louis' name was the better known. So the band was put in his name.

Everyone was short of cash, although Louis said that he had just sold a book of trumpet exercises to Melrose, the music publishers, for $200. The book came out in 1927. Four of the bandsmen, including Louis and Dickerson had cars. It was agreed that each man would bring $20 for finances during the trip. Liz stayed behind, but was to act as treasurer. Zutty Singleton recalled: "We loaded all the stuff in the car. Finally Lil made a loan on something and got $20 for each of us. That was some trip. We had a couple of vibraphones—tied them on the car and they got all rusty. We didn't know enough to make stops, to play. Louis was really coming then, but we didn't stop. When we got to New York, we didn't have nothing. Next morning [Wellman] Braud helped us out."

The band members who made the trip included pianist Gene Anderson, saxophonists Crawford Wethington, Bert Curry and Jimmy Strong, trumpeter Homer Hobson, trombonist Fred Robinson, Mancy Carr on banjo, bassist Peter Briggs, Zutty Singleton, Carroll Dickerson on swing violin, and Louis.

The little caravan barnstormed its way across the country, making stops in Detroit, Dayton and Cleveland. When the cars reached Buffalo somebody thought it would be nice to see Niagara Falls, and so the detour was taken. Zutty drove Louis' Hupmobile, the same one

Robert Goffin said was stolen; apparently it had been recovered, stripped of almost everything useful. Louis spent most of his time on a trip east sleeping in the back seat.

Each city they visited greeted the band enthusiastically, for Louis' name was well known from the radio broadcasts. They visited cabarets in each city and soon discovered that their reputation was far greater than any of the bandsmen had dreamed. Wherever there were musicians, the travelers were invited to sit in and play a few numbers. There was never a check to pick up afterward.

With a little advance planning, the trip could have been profitable; but no one had thought to make such bookings, a shortsightedness a manager could have avoided. Apparently Louis did not at that time have a manager.

Carroll Dickerson's Marmon failed to make it all of the way to New York. The car was involved in a collision in a small town in the middle west and there abandoned, the passengers distributed among the other three vehicles. With the instruments and the luggage, all three cars must have been seriously overloaded.

And when the caravan at last reached New York City and Times Square, the Hupmobile chose that famous spot to blow its radiator cap. A traffic cop walked over and studied the disreputable looking trio of out of state vehicles, read the Illinois plates and gave them a cold look. Anyone from Chicago was viewed with suspicion on the part of law enforcement officers in the rest of the country. The cop told them to move on, which they were glad to do.

Tommy Rockwell was less than happy to discover that he had an entire band on his hands, although he promised to do what he could. The band played a few dates at the Audobon Theatre, substituting for Duke Ellington; and then at the Savoy Ballroom.

In late May Louis went to Philadelphia for a brief reunion with Fletcher Henderson, whose band was the orchestra for the Youmans show. The New York Age, a black newspaper, reported that Louis was supposed to have been first cornetist and Russell Smith, second cornetist. After one number had been played, Louis was told to change chairs with Smith. The number was replayed, and the decision made that Louis was not adapted to the Broadway stage.

The reunion ended with the first rehearsal, although it is doubtful that Henderson was the one to turn thumbs down on Louis. He returned to New York and by June was leading the band at the Savoy, with Carroll Dickerson as musical director. Then came an engagement for the band at Connie's Inn in Harlem, which along with Small's and the Cotton Club, were the leading Harlem clubs of the time.

Connie Immerman, owner of Connie's Inn, was at that time producing "Hot Chocolates," the first all-black Broadway revue. He had taken his regular band, Leroy Smith's Orchestra, downtown for the revue. Louis doubled up with Smith on Broadway, where he was given a feature number of his own to both play and sing. The number was a new song written by Fats Waller and Andy Razaf, *Ain't Misbehavin'*. It was an immediate success for both Louis and the composers, and the most famous number to come out of the show.

The Harlem clubs didn't start up until after the downtown theaters let out, about midnight; they stayed open until morning. The customers had to wear evening clothes or they were turned away. It was still the time of

Prohibition, of course, but even without booze a couple could easily spend $40 to $60 a night. Many brought their own flasks and bought splits of ginger ale at a dollar a bottle. Booze was available under the table at $10 a pint or more. The cover charge was $7 to $10 a person, and Louis later remembered that an order of chicken a la king was $3, a cup of black coffee, forty cents. This was in a time when a college student graduate might earn $30 a week, a laborer much less.

The Connie's Inn job lasted about four months, until the Leroy Smith orchestra returned. Rockwell had been booking Louis as a solo attraction on the side; he had guested several times with Luis Russell's band. He also did a two-month gig at New York's Coconut Grove with the Mills Blue Rhythm Band, led by drummer William Lynch.

When Connie's Inn folded, the Dickerson band broke up; many of them returned to Chicago. Louis took the Mills Blue Rhythm Band on a road trip to Detroit, Baltimore, Philadelphia, Pittsburgh and Chicago, fronting it. When the trip was finished, he returned to New York.

The stop in Baltimore was at the Royal Theatre. It was the middle of winter, and the theater was located in a poor black neighborhood. It was freezing cold, the people were so poor they couldn't afford hard coal. Louis ordered a ton of coal and had it delivered to the lobby of the theater, where the poor were permitted to help themselves. Afterward, they came backstage to thank him in what he later said was one of the proudest moments of his life, knowing he had helped those who needed it most.

At this time, Louis decided to travel west and received a booking at Frank Sebastian's New Cotton Club in

Culver City, California. He stopped in Chicago for a visit and then took off to California.

In 1929 Louis began to change his repertoire, recording some of the popular songs of the day. The Hot 5 and the Hot 7 recordings were known in black areas and to other musicians, but received almost no acceptance from the public at large. The audience for jazz continued to shrink, the sweet music of the big bands taking over.

Ain't Misbehavin' was Louis' first big popular hit, although he had recorded *I Can't Give You Anything But Love* a few months earlier. Juke boxes were growing in popularity at this time, and helped spread his reputation even further. Some musicians think that Louis' peak period was from 1925 through 1928, but it is a fact that those who refused to adapt to the changing tastes in music soon found themselves forgotten. During the early thirties, Louis was virtually the only black jazz artist to continue recording.

It has been said that Louis made the trip west because his personal life was becoming more and more difficult. He had quarreled with Zutty, and by early summer relations with Lil were really strained. Robert Goffin claims that on the last night of Louis' gig at Connie's Inn, a familiar face appeared in the audience: Fanny.

They got together after the show because Fanny was scheduled to leave for Paris in the morning. The parting apparently was bittersweet, Louis thankful to be rid of one problem but honestly missing her.

Goffin also reported that during the run of "Hot Chocolates," Louis received an unprecedented honor. Famous white band leader Ben Pollack was in the audience one Sunday, along with a delegation of show business greats. When the performance ended, Pollack came out of the audience and presented Louis with a watch. The inscription read: *Good luck always to Louis Armstrong/From the Musicians of Broadway.*

Lil Armstrong said, about the trip to California: "That's when things started going oozy-woozy. We weren't agreeing on anything."

Whenever Louis had problems with his life he looked forward to travel as a means of escape. Now he looked forward to seeing what his reception would be on the west coast. Frank Sebastian's New Cotton Club had opened in 1927. Culver City is one of the many towns making up greater Los Angeles and rather a dreary place today. Apparently then it was a suburb to Hollywood.

Louis appeared in front of a house orchestra led first by trumpeter Vernon Elkins. Les Hite took over after a short time. In the band were twenty-two year old trombonist Lawrence Brown and twenty-one year old drummer, Lionel Hampton. Hampton idolized Louis; and in return, Louis rated Hamp as a first class drummer from the start.

As did most percussionists, Hampton already played the xylophone and marimbas; but Louis convinced him to try the vibraphone as well. Hampton remembered: "We used to hear all the other bands on records; then we'd taken down all their parts and play 'em. All the big movie stars and everything came out there; so they brought Louis Armstrong in to be the star of the show. . .this really was a great experience for me, playing behind Louis. This started me playing the vibes because I made a recording session with him, and when I went to the studio there were some vibes in the corner. At that time drummers were just striking one note occasionally on the vibes, as it was fairly new. And Louis said, 'Play something on that.' By me knowing the percussion, I thought of playing jazz, right there on the keyboard. . . Then I made an introduction with Louis on the vibraharp, and that was the first time four hammers were ever played.''

Louis made many records on the west coast, including the earlier mentioned back-up session with Jimmie Rodgers. Some critics considered some of the sax passages on these cuts cloying, but they were the direct result of Louis' admiration for Guy Lombardo.

''When we were at the Savoy in Chicago in 1928,'' Louis remembered, ''every Saturday night we'd catch the Owl Club, with Guy Lombardo, and as long as he played we'd sit right there. . . We didn't go nowhere until after Lombardo signed off. That went on for months.''

In California, Louis met and signed on with manager Johnny Collins, although nothing is known about Collins' background. In 1976, ABC-TV presented a movie of the week, ''Louis Armstrong: Chicago-Style.'' Collins was played by Red Buttons. Ben Vereen was Louis and Janet McLachlan, Lil Hardin Armstrong.

Reviewing the movie in *TV Guide*, Judith Crist thought it was a muddled melodrama of Louis' career through the twenties and early thirties. However, she praised Vereen for his performance, for his singing in a gravel-throated voice of Louis' songs, and for the first-rate jazz performed on the soundtrack.

Louis' managers were less happy with the movie, for they had sold the rights to his life story in 1970, to Audio Fidelity Enterprises for a guaranteed half-million dollars against royalties. A.F.E was the parent company of Audio Fidelity Records. In 1974, the rights were sold to Paramount, for a movie to star Flip Wilson. Apparently the TV movie killed that project. In 1977, the rights were sold again, a new deal negotiated with Universal. At this writing, nothing has happened on the project, at least for public announcement.

Louis stayed at the New Cotton Club for nine happy months, through the spring of 1931. Robert Goffin says that all through this period Fanny kept sending him cables, begging Louis to join her in Paris. Alpha also wrote him a series of heartbreaking letters, and at last came out on the train. According to Goffin, Lil was there at the same time, although she had a romantic interest of her own: a masseur she was seeing on the side. Lil shortly returned to Chicago, taking the masseur with her.

Speaking of Alpha, Lil Armstrong said: "Don't know when or how long Louis had an affair with Alpha. I can assure you she was not the only one, so I didn't worry too much about it."

Louis himself said: "Four women I married and none of them ain't hurt me yet. They must have loved me. They all proved something, said something, and they all gave me a lot of experience you couldn't get nowhere else. All my wives got the best that's in me."

During this trip, Louis made his first movies. According to Hugues Pannasie, the first was a Betty Boop cartoon, in which Louis appeared in animation, singing *I'll Be Glad When You're Dead You Rascal You*. He also made a one-reel musical short for Paramount, in which Louis and the band dressed up in tiger skins and played the same song, and also *Shine*.

None of the books about Louis mention his first feature motion picture, "Ex-Flame," made for the independent Tiffany Company. The movie was adapted from "East Lynne," a soap-opera novel by Mrs. Henry

Wood which was immensely popular some years earlier, and starred, among others, famous silent movie comedian Snub Pollard and Neil Hamilton, who later became most famous for playing the role of the police commission in the "Batman" TV series.

Dates given in the filmography at the end of this book are the years of release. If Pannasie is right, and the Betty Boop cartoon was first, then it was apparently held back until 1932. On his 1933 trip to Europe, Louis appeared in a Danish movie but did not appear in another Hollywood production until 1936, when he was in Bing Crosby's "Pennies From Heaven." From 1936 on, Louis made many films.

It was common practice in Hollywood musicals made in the 1930s and 1940s for any black musicians or singers to be presented in such a way that their performance could be cut by Southern states censors without affecting the story line. Blacks were never presented in anything but a musical role or as a figure of farce. In 1943 Louis played the Devil's helper in "Cabin In the Sky," which was perhaps the first white-made movie to present a black story in a completely sympathetic and serious manner. However, it was not until "A Man Called Adam" in 1966 that he was given the chance to play his first truly dramatic role, that of an aging jazz singer.

After nine months at the Cotton Club in Culver City, Louis had a run-in with the law and ended up spending the next nine days in the Los Angeles County Jail. It was not until the end of his life that he told the full story of what had happened in a very long letter to Max Jones. The letter was published in full in Jones' *Louis*.

Jazz musicians have always been accused, with a great deal of justice, of being 'dopers,' and users of marijuana. Long before grass and other recreational drugs became accepted by millions, the early users were referred to as "vipers." Marijuana was called tea, muggles, or reefers; and much early jazz contains references to the weed. Jones quoted as examples, Mezz Mezzrow's *Sendin' the Vipers,* Stuff Smith's *If You're a Viper,* Fats Waller's *Viper Rag.* Other song titles of the day include *Golden Leaf Strut, Muggles, Texas Tea Party, Chant of the Weed, Song of the Vipers,* and *Smoking Reefers.* Some of the top black artists, including Louis, made such recordings, among whom were Cab Calloway, Earl Hines, Duke Ellington and Wingy Manone.

Louis said: ". . .we did call ourselves Vipers. . .it was a misdemeanor in those days. . . .Vic Berton (the top drummer then in all Hollywood) and I got busted together. It was during our intermission which were packed and jammed every night with all sorts of my fans, including movie stars. . .Vic and I were blasting this joint. . .Just then two big healthy Dicks came from behind a car—nonchalantly—and said to us, we'll take the roach, boys. . . . So one Dick stayed with me until. . .I did my last show, he enjoyed it too. . .Then this Dick confidentially told me. . .this wouldn't have happened if that band leader. . .who's playing just up the road from you, and the big name that he's supposed to have, didn't get jealous. . .So dropped a nickel on you. . .into the telephone. . .

". . .I spent nine days in the Downtown Los Angeles City Jail, in a cell with two guys who were already sentenced to forty or forty-five years for something else. . .So I got to trial. Everybody were there. . .my boss, manager and a whole gang of lawyers. . .Meantime the Chicago papers were all on the stands with big headlines saying Louis Armstrong will have to serve six months for marijuana. . .The judge gave me a suspended sentence and I went to work that night. . .Mary Warner, honey, you sure was good and I enjoyed you 'heep much.' But the price got a little too high to pay (law wise.) At first you was a 'misdomeanor.' But as the years rolled on you lost your misdo and got meanor and meanor . . .''

Louis left Los Angeles in March, 1931, and returned to Chicago, where Johnny Collins had booked him into a newly-remodeled club, the Showboat. He formed a new band for this engagement, with Charlie Alexander on piano, Preston Jackson, trombone, Mike McKendricks, banjo, Fred "Tubby" Hall on drums, George James on first alto sax, Lester Boone, second alto sax, Al Washington, tenor sax, Zilner T. Randolph as second trumpet and Johnny Lindsay on bass violin. With this band he recorded for OKeh; some of his earlier recordings had been done for Victor.

It was at this time Louis had his trouble mentioned at the beginning of this chapter. However, first Chicago staged a tumultuous welcome for him on his opening night. According to Robert Goffin, the band played all night, every half hour a noted white jazzman stepping to the microphone to read a special tribute to Louis. In the audience that night were members of the orchestras of Paul Whiteman and Ted Lewis, Eddie Condon, Jean Goldkette and Bing Crosby.

Alpha was also in the audience, but a little later Lil arrived and took a seat just five tables away from Alpha. Alpha managed to hide behind a handerkerchief and made a quick exit.

A story in the April 25, 1931 issue of the black Chicago newspaper, *The Chicago Defender*, announced

that Messrs. Weil, Fiore and Ryan had been arrested for
trying to extort $6,000 to $10,000 from Louis. Robert
Goffin said that mobster Frank Foster waited in Louis'
dressing room, wearing a false beard and carrying a pistol. When Louis came into the room, Foster told him
that he was leaving for New York to play a date at
Connie's Inn.

Louis objected that his manager had told him nothing
about such a date, and Foster told him to forget about
Johnny Collins. Louis was told to telephone New York
and confirm the Connie's Inn date. He did so, and
Foster left. Collins arrived a short time later with the
cops and admitted that he had trouble with New York.

Johnny Collins told Louis that he had a theater date
in Chicago for him for two months, but Louis said no.
He would not go to New York, nor would he stay in
Chicago. Instead, he took the band out on a road trip
that lasted ten months before it was done at last and
took them through fifty or sixty cities and towns. Along
the way was a return to New Orleans, the first time he
had been home in nine years.

When the Goffin book was published in 1947, he
implicated Tommy Rockwell in the situation. Rockwell
sued Goffin's publisher for defamation of character,
and in a *Downbeat* interview gave his version of the
events. He had been in Chicago with Dave Kapp of
Decca Records and, in his hotel room, was told by four
men to get out of town within four hours. This made
him mad, and so Rockwell went to the Showboat and
tried to see Louis. Failing in that, he caught the train
back to New York the next morning.

Rockwell had acted as Louis' manager before the
California trip. Chicago, of course, was ruled by the
mobs, with Al Capone the overlord of all. Preston Jack-

son, the band's trombonist, remembered one fight between rival gangs at the Showboat when guns began blasting. Tubby Hall hid under the piano and the rest of the band dived for cover, but Louis continued playing.

It was reported in June that members of the orchestra had been expelled from the American Federation of Musicians for continuing to play with Louis after he had been expelled from the union for not fulfilling a contract with New York night club. This must have been Connie's Inn. New York City newspapers in December reported that the court case of Louis Armstrong vs. Connie Immerman and Tommy Rockwell was due to be heard on December 15. No results of the hearing were ever published, so it has been assumed that the case was settled out of court.

In the meantime, Collins booked the southern tour that brought Louis to New Orleans early in June. The last of the magnolias were still on the trees, and when the train pulled into the old L & N station by the Mississippi, Louis heard hot music. Eight bands, headed by the Zulu Club band, were there to greet him with a tremendous crowd. When Louis got off the train they picked him up and carried him on their shoulders down the center of Canal Street.

Many of Louis' old friends were there to greet him, including Captain Jones and Peter Davis of the Waif's Home. The next day he went down to the Home, where he was an instant hit with the boys. However, many others had moved on. Kid Ory was in California, Zutty in Chicago; Fate Marable had left the river and was in St. Louis. He did see David Jones, for a happy reunion.

From June through August the band was booked into the prestigious Suburban Gardens, where it broadcast every night. On opening night, the Gardens were surrounded by an estimated ten thousand blacks, who had gathered in the hopes of hearing the music through the open windows. There were another five thousand whites inside; but when it came for the white announcer to introduce Louis, he refused to do so, and walked off the stage.

For a moment the situation was tense; then Louis took over the introduction himself and continued to do so through the run of the show. He was reunited with his sister on this trip and with the rest of his family. But his own people were locked out of the hall.

On his last night in New Orleans, Louis had arranged to perform a concert without pay at a nearby Army base. But when he started for the base that night, he found crowds of people turned back and the gates of the base locked. Soldiers armed with fix bayonets stood guard.

There was never an explanation of why the concert was cancelled, but Louis left town the next morning with bitter memories. The tour contined into Texas.

Robert Goffin says that Alpha was with Louis on the trip, booked into a black hotel. The situation became tense again when Lil arrived, towing, according to Goffin, her masseur. She managed to get into Louis' bedroom, where they had a knockdown fight that lasted for hours. The next morning Louis found that Lil had gone with his car.

Lil Armstrong says that she was still trying to save the marriage at this time, hoping for a reconciliation; but Louis had decided on divorce. However, the divorce took seven years to come through, at last allowing Louis to marry Alpha.

In New Orleans, Louis sponsored a local baseball team, buying them new uniforms that said Armstrong across the shirt front. The team was known as Armstrong's Secret Nine. At the same time a cigar company was marketing a Louis Armstrong Special.

Johnny Collins' wife was in charge of transportation for the tour; she had chartered a new Greyhound bus, to escape the dirty Jim Crow coaches found throughout the South. When the bus pulled into Memphis, Mrs. Collins was sitting up front, the only white person aboard. This attracted immediate unpopular attention. The police were called, and the entire band and Mrs. Collins arrested, charged with refusing to change buses for their next destination.

Johnny Collins secured their release with the promise that Louis would play a broadcast. The place was so crowded that Louis remembered having to climb over people sitting on the floor to get to the bandstand. The first number was dedicated to the Memphis Chief of Police, who was present, as Louis swung into *I'll Be Glad When You're Dead You Rascal You.*

The band next played five weeks in St. Louis, then began to work it's way north. At the end of the year they were in Philadelphia, and then in January, the problem with Rockwell and Connie Immerman settled, they moved to the Lafayette Theatre in Harlem. From there, they went out again, returning to Chicago in March, where Louis disbanded the group.

Louis himself returned to California for another engagement at the New Cotton Club, where the orchestra was still under the direction of Les Hite. But he was tired; he needed a change, something new. He decided to go to Europe.

He bought a Buick (an old one, according to *Swing That Music.* However, in the Meryman interview, he mentioned owning a $3,200 Buick that he sold in bad times for $300. According to the "Encyclopedia of American Cars 1930 to 1942," the most expensive Buick of the entire decade was never priced more than a few dollars above $2,000) Louis drove the Buick east, stopping in Chicago to clear up a few details; and then he went on to New York.

In July, with Alpha and Mr. and Mrs. Johnny Collins, Louis boarded the White Star Line's *Majestic* and set sail for England.

10
TRAVELIN' ON

10

Travelin' On

The trip to Europe was hastily arranged and poorly prepared. An eager reception awaited Louis, for there had been several previous jazz bands before him. Sidney Bechet had toured Britain as early as 1918 with the Southern Syncopated Orchestra, and about the same time the Original Dixieland Jazz Bend went over. In 1925, Red McKenzie's Mound City Blue Blowers had been successful; and in 1930, Jimmy Dorsey had toured with Ted Lewis, and Bunny Berigan with Hal Kemp.

The timing was right. The hard core audience of jazz enthusiasts was strong enough to support such a tour; just three years later would have been too late, because in 1935 England's Ministry of Labour established a ban that effectively kept foreign jazz musicians out of the country for the next twenty years. After Louis left England at the close of his second European tour in 1934, he did not return again until 1956.

The Melody had been asking Louis to come for some time, because his playing was perhaps at the peak of his career. American musicians were known from their records. The European radio stations of the time devoted little play time to popular music. Instead, the air waves were filled with the classics and with lectures.

The Europeans had taken jazz to their hearts because only the best music was imported. The trashy music of the imitators that flooded American never got beyond the shores. Duke Ellington and Cab Calloway had also toured Europe to a great deal of success.

Louis received a radiogram on the *Majestic* that a banquet would be held in his honor that Friday night at the Ambassador. However, only Londoner Dan Ingman managed to make it to Paddington Station to meet the 12:25 a.m. boat train from Plymouth. Louis was accompanied by a large white man with a cigar in his mouth and by two women; apparently Alpha's mother had come along. Since Louis was having problems with Lil, it has not been explained who was taking care of Clarence, who must have been about seventeen.

Collins introduced Louis and Alpha as Mr. and Mrs. Armstrong. Ingman remembered later that Louis wore a purple suit, an enormous white cap and a long tan coat. They had no landing permits, but somehow Collins had talked them ashore. There had been no arrangements made for a hotel, and so Ingman was forced to get on the telephone in the early hours and start calling around London.

He began with the most famous hotels of the day, and quickly worked down to second-rate. Some simply had no room; others he thought it best to warn that there were blacks and whites together in the party. The answer was always no, while Louis' group stood on the train platform, surrounded by piles of luggage.

Finally Ingman remembered an exclusive hotel in Norfolk Street, off the Strand; and the answer was yes. The hotel was the Howard, and the staff showed the party the utmost courtesy when they arrived despite the lateness of the hour. Louis needed a trumpet repairer, and Ingman promised to send one around first thing in the morning. He went home, after first alerting a few people to where the Armstrong party was staying and at last fell into bed.

The next morning a bombshell hit the hotel as reporters and fans descended upon the premises. At last the Howard complained, and a few days later the party moved out. Officially, Johnny Collins said that the Howard was too expensive, but they may well have been asked to leave.

Nat Gonella, the young English jazzman, was in Boosey and Hawkes' store when he learned that Louis' trumpet was about to be returned. Gonella begged the errand, and when he arrived at the hotel, refused to hand the instrument over to anyone but Louis. In that way he got to meet his idol for the first time, Louis granting him half an hour.

The banquet was to be that evening, but the luggage had not yet arrived from Paddington Station. Louis had only the suit he was wearing. An emergency was arranged, and the party left for the Ambassador. Most of the top musicians in England were present, including band leaders Ray Noble and Billy Cotton. Some of the musicians questioned Louis closely, thinking that he had not managed to hit the high C notes on his records but had done it with a clarinet. They examined his mouthpiece, expecting a trick, but still weren't satisfied until he took one of their trumpets and demonstrated his powers. Then they cheered him.

Louis was overwhelmed by his reception at the banquet, for he did not realize how popular his records were there. Because arrangements had been so sloppy, it was necessary to bring in several black musicians from Paris to put together a pickup band. Among them were Joe Hayman, Fletcher Allen, Charlie Johnson, and an old friend from New Orleans, Peter du Conge. Louis had to speak to several of them through an interpreter, and it has been said that at least two of the slots had to be filled locally.

There was little time to rehearse, but during the rehearsal, Johnny Collins showed up drunk. Apparently he had been trying to make up for twelve years of Prohibition in America in one day. He quarreled with Louis and started to leave—walking into a plate glass window instead of the revolving door. His dignity, his cigar, and his nose were crushed.

On the day of the premiere at the Palladium, Fanny showed up at the door of Louis' suite. She had made a special trip from Paris by plane. Alpha was there at the time, and the situation was tense as Louis introduced Alpha as his fiancee. Fanny left, bitter, leaving an angry Alpha behind.

That evening, as they neared the Palladium, Alpha saw a taxi and though the open window, Fanny. That made her boil over again. Just before Louis was to go on stage, she tried to strangle him, according to Robert Goffin, ripping the lapel off his coat. Louis tried to shake her off, and at last had to drop her with one uppercut. He found another coat and ran on stage; but when he came back to the dressing room, Alpha was still out cold. The Collins tried to revive her while Louis ran back for an encore, and when he returned again, she was sitting up, groggy but conscious.

The Palladium was sold out for the entire two week run, but Louis was not exactly what their regular paying customers expected. Some of the older patrons started to walk out early in the evening. Nat and Bruts Gonella, brothers, were sitting in the audience at every show, and they remembered trying in the darkness to trip those leaving.

Still, the run was successful, breaking a house record. On the last day, the management of the Palladium presented Louis with a gold Selmer trumpet with his name engraved on it. In *Swing That Music*, four years later, he said that it was his favorite instrument, played all the time.

At this time Louis met Hugues Pannasie and Robert Goffin, who had come over from France and Belgium. Louis had lost a great deal of weight and was actually slim; the photographs of the tour show him as slender.

After the Palladium run, Louis went on a tour of England and Scotland. The black band had to return to Paris, and so he put together a ten-piece white group that included among others Lou Davis, Billie Mason, Allan Ferguson, Buddie Featherstonhaugh, Len Berman and Bruts Gonella. Mason was the leader, and he recalled years later his surprise and embarrassment to learn that he was earning more than Louis did as star.

Both Panassie and Goffin had published books on jazz criticism. Louis was pleased to discover that Goffin's was dedicated to 'Louis Armstrong, the Real King of Jazz, in testimony of my high admiration.' He began a correspondence with both that lasted for many years.

The white group was much better than the first, probably because he had his pick of better musicians. Toward the end of the tour, however, it was said that this group was replaced by another white band, which was much inferior.

Part of the criticism directed toward Louis was that he was too much of a showman. Back in America, his audiences were thrilled when he made an effort to reach a hundred or more high C's in a row; but to the English audiences, it came as a shock. He had already begun the practice of having a batch of twenty or forty freshly laundered and starched handkerchiefs on hand for each performance; this may have begun in 1926 or 1927, and was well-established by 1929. Children in the street would run up to him with a handkerchief tied around their hand to show how much they loved him, according to Mezz Mezzrow. There were stories of Louis' changing handkerchiefs as many as six times in one number.

When Louis returned to England in 1956, for the Hungarian Relief Fund, another banquet was given for him at the same Ambassador. Only Dave Toff and Buddy Featherstonhaugh managed to make it both times, although Nat Gonella sent his regrets from the north of Scotland.

The tour was successful, although Dan Ingram reported that one night when the band was ready to play, Johnny Collins demanded the money up front, in cash. The promoter offered a check, which Collins turned down; the man was forced to go to the box office and returned with several bags of half crowns and other silver. Collins couldn't even count the English coins, but he announced that he was satisfied. Louis sat through the episode in obvious embarrassment, his trumpet dangling from his fingers but he was too much of a gentleman to say anything.

Louis' earnings on the tour are unknown, but he seemed to have little left after catering to Alpha's taste for fine clothes and late nights. A few years later, when he was earning only $75 a night, he told someone that Alpha's fondness for furs and diamonds had him constantly paying on time.

When the tour ended, Louis went to Paris for a week, for what he said was a chance to rest up. According to others, dates were offered, but Johnny Collins demanded so much money that no one could meet his price.

So they returned to New York, landing, according to Louis, on November 2, 1932—the day Franklin D. Roosevelt was elected President of the United States. However, Bill Mather claimed that the actual date was a week later, on November 9. Mather said he met Louis two hours after landing and took him to Connie's Inn, where he was introduced from the floor to a big welcome.

At the end of that month, Louis appeared in a revival of "Hot Chocolates," with Chick Webb's band, taking the show on tour until the middle of January. During the tour he suffered with sore lips. Mezz Mezzrow, in his book *Really the Blues,* and Louis' lip was so bad "it looked like he had a big overgrown strawberry sitting on it."

One night, playing *Them There Eyes*, the lip split. The song finished with a high F, and Louis struggled to make it. Charlie Green, the trombonist, left the stage and burst into tears. Chick Webb, also crying, did what he could on the drums to help out. Face bleeding and perspiring, Louis was almost on hands and knees when he finished the song; but finish it he did.

174 Louis Armstrong: Biography of a Musician

After the "Hot Chocolates" tour, Louis returned to Chicago, where his first move was to find a big pot of red beans and rice. Then he went to hear Earl Hines. He then formed a new band, with Zilner T. Randolph as leader, Budd Johnson on tenor sax, Keg Johnson on trombone, and the almost unknown Teddy Wilson as pianist. In Chicago, he stayed with Alpha's mother.

There were no record dates on this trip, because both Victor and Columbia claimed his exclusive services. In the meantime, in England the Daily Express ran a story on the first page of its March 31 edition that Louis had died from overexertion. Calls and letters flooded the newspapers and the offices of the Melody Maker from all over the country, and on April 4, the music magazine received a cable from Spike Hughes that Louis had been bitten by a dog and was in fine shape.

Louis toured with the new band until July, when a deal fell through for a summer engagement at the Pabst Blue Ribbon Casino in Chicago. Louis disbanded the group and decided to return to England. This time he would stay eighteen months before he returned home again.

At the end of July, 1933, Louis opened at London's Holborn Empire Theatre, this time with a deliberately commercial show that offended many of his jazz fans. However, the show received a greater acceptance from the general public.

Johnny Collins had returned to England with him, but Louis had troubles with his manager. The Melody Maker reported on August 19 that Collins and Louis had parted company. Louis told Richard Meryman that he woke up one morning to find that his manager had sailed with his passport, stranding him.

Something had happened to Louis during the past

year. Earlier, he always seemed ready to give in to others, do whatever they wanted. However, on this second trip he started standing up for himself. It has been speculated that Alpha may have had some influence, but this is uncertain. Others think that she was too much in love with the bright lights and late nights to worry about other aspects of Louis' career.

Jack Hylton took over as his temporary manager, and it was reported that Louis was considering settling permanently in England. In October he crossed the English Channel to make his first appearances in Scandanavia and Holland. It was said that ten thousand screaming people greeted him on his arrival in Copenhagen. It was apparently at this time that he made his contribution to "Copenhagen Kalundborg," which was a filmed revue featuring top performers of the day. Louis and his orchestra performed three numbers in the film.

On Johnny Collins: Louis told Richard Meryman that Collins was always in trouble with the promoters, always trying to make Louis declare bankruptcy. But he gave no hint as to where Collins had come from or why he had signed with him in the first place. Collins was continually coming up with publicity stunts that Louis felt were bad for his image as well as his career.

Reviewers in England felt that both his health and his playing improved with Collins gone. At the end of the year Louis received a cable from Collins offering lucrative engagements in New York, but Louis crumpled the wire in his hands and dropped it on the floor of his dressing room, saying, "Never, never, never!"

Back in London in December, Louis toured England again until April 1934; and then he moved to Paris for a long vacation. He rented a furnished apartment and lazed around for three or four months. Louis obviously appreciated the freedom of Paris, which had no color line. He was welcomed everywhere he went in Europe, with the exception of Nazi Germany. During his eighteen months, he was received by the King of the Belgians, the crown Prince of Sweden and King Umberto of Italy. He played at least one concert in front of the Prince of Wales and his brother, George; and another in front of George V. At the latter, about to play *I'll Be Glad When Your Dead, You Rascal You,* he called up to the Royal Box: "I'm gonna dedicate this one for you, Rex." Almost everyone was horrified, but the King of England laughed heartily.

While in Paris, Louis cut six sides—the first records he had made since leaving the United States in 1933. One side was deleted within a few days of its release— *Song of the Vipers*—when the record company found out what vipers were.

Agent N. J Canetti booked Louis through Belgium, France, Italy and Switzerland on a tour that lasted until early January. Apparently it was cut short because Louis was having lip troubles, which caused bitterness. In *Swing That Music* he recalled playing for the Crown Princess of Italy in Turin and spending New Year's Eve in Lausanne, Switzerland, after crossing the Alps by bus. On the latter trip they saw an Italian Army ski patrol skiiing down a mountainside, which impressed them greatly.

Jack Hylton wanted to team Louis with Coleman Hawkins for a super spectacular jazz concert on April 22 of that year, but after the publicity was released Louis refused to play. Hawkins appeared alone, to a great triumph. Many people thought Louis had walked out in an attack of artistic temperament, but years later he said that Hawkins thought that he, Louis, wasn't big enough to share a billing with him. So the deal was bull from the start.

Agent Canetti claimed Louis had breached a contract, that he had exclusive rights to his services; but Louis had also signed a contract with English agent Audrey Thacker which had precedence. To avoid further problems, he returned to New York in late January, 1935, after an eighteen month absence.

Apparently his lips were still bothering Louis, but a deal had been made for him to once again take out the Chick Webb band. Johnny Collins secured an injunction stopping the engagement. In the Richard Meryman interview, Louis said that he paid Collins $5,000 to buy off the contract. The agent dropped from sight; he was last heard from in Florida, about 1960. Attempts to trace him after that were unsuccessful.

Louis returned to Chicago and paid a visit to Joe Glaser, during which he convinced Glaser to become his manager. He laid off for six months, apparently at the advice of his doctors, although he sang one night with the Duke Ellington Orchestra and again at an American Federation of Musicians tribute to Louis. A British magazine reported at this time that Louis was to be managed by Mezz Mezzrow, but nothing ever came of it. He relaxed in his South Parkway apartment with his two dogs and knocked around with Zutty Singleton, trying to forget his problems. By that time Lil had filed suit for $6,000 in back maintenance, so his problems were mounting.

Joe Glaser apparently was reluctant to take on Louis' managerial chores, but he gave up all of his other business and traveled with Louis from then on, driving his Cadillac four hundred to five hundred miles a day through the South. Glaser finally opened a small office in the Rockwell & O'Keefe Building in New York. He had booked the biggest acts into his clubs, and now he was booking Louis, so he decided that he might as well take on other clients. In time, his Associated Booking Company became the biggest booking agency in the country, and today, the estate of Louis Armstrong is still represented by the company, although Glaser died in 1969. But Louis was his first client.

Louis no longer had to worry about the headaches of keeping a band: payroll, watching the box office, commissions, taxes, picking songs to record. Glaser gave him a monthly allowance and took care of everything else. Now he could concentrate on his music, which from the first was the only thing that was really important to him.

Apparently money problems were severe during this layoff; it must have been then that he sold his Buick for $300. However, he had brought one cherished souvenir back from England: a medieval trumpet, presented by a fan whose family had owned the instrument since the middle ages. Louis liked to play the crude horn, wondering what songs it had played over the centuries.

In June, Louis put together a new band, led by Zilner T. Randolph, for a tour of the western and southern states. There was another triumphal return to New Orleans, and the tour ended in New York in September. The members of the band were unable to get union cards to perform in New York, and so the unit was disbanded. Louis played Connie's Inn, which had moved downtown to Broadway with the Luis Russell Orchestra. About this time Joe Glaser took over management of the Russell band, which stayed with Louis for the next several years.

At Connie's Inn, Louis broadcast over a coast-to-coast CBS radio network hookup. This was the time when swing was coming into its own and big bands almost dominated the airways. Apparently at this time he wrote *Swing That Music*, which was published the next year. The next summer, Louis had his tonsils out at a cost of $400.

He also had a new contract, with Decca, and recorded frequently. Jack Kapp, the president of Decca, was always experimenting with his recording artists, and at different times had Louis accompanied by a white studio orchestra with Bunny Berigan on second trumpet, by Jimmy Dorsey's band, and by a five-piece group, the Polynesians.

Between 1936 and 1939, Louis made seven trips to California, during which he made many of his films. "Pennies from Heaven" was an enjoyable experience, and when the film was completed, Bing Crosby presented Louis with a money clip with a watch inserted in it. Louis treasured this for many years. Playing the Royal Theatre in Baltimore, he thought he had lost it; but it turned out that someone had borrowed it while he wasn't looking. Louis was frantic, and had the place in an uproar, when the miscreant returned the clip. After that, it was never allowed from his sight.

Over the years, Louis continued to record with other artists, including Bing Crosby, Frances Langford, the Mills Brothers, the Casa Loma Band, Ella Fitzgerald, Andy Iona and His Islanders, Billie Holiday, Duke Ellington, the Dukes of Dixieland, and too many more to list. He did not know that Joe Glaser had insured his life for $100,000. Glaser insured himself for the same amount, with Louis as beneficiary.

In January, 1937, Louis had another bout of surgery

for a minor throat ailment, then went on tour with the Russell band, crisscrossing the country. In April he started a radio series for Fleischmann's Yeast, and then went through the South. In Savannah, Georgia, he ran into an old friend—Joe Oliver.

Oliver's days of glory were over. After Louis left him in Chicago, his career had begun a steady downward drift. He tried New York but was told he was past his prime. He took out small groups on one-nighters, but was forced to hire inexperienced youngsters. Louis told Richard Meryman how these young men used to hurry to the boarding house dinner table and eat up all of the food before Joe came down, then laugh at him.

Oliver had a little vegetable stand in Savannah. He shed no tears for what had been; he was just happy to see Louis again. Louis and the others in the band emptied their pockets for him, and that night Joe showed up in the wings dressed like the Joe Oliver of 1915: Stetson hat turned down, high-button shoes, box-back coat. He had redeemed his good clothes from pawn.

Louis did what he could for Joe while he was in Savannah, although he himself was only making $75 a night at the time. Alpha's expensive tastes made it hard for him to save anything. After the band left Georgia, an old Oliver fan gave Joe a job cleaning out a bar, cleaning the spittoons on which he used to beat out his tempo.

Oliver died soon after, from what was said to be a heart attack. Louis knew it was a broken heart. The body was brought to New York by the Actors Fund, and every musician who could make it was there. Louis paid his visit, but had to leave to go to work.

Louis felt that Joe Oliver never received the break that Bunk Johnson got. Bunk was found working in a cotton field by promoters who brought him back to the city, brought him store teeth and new clothes. Bunk was still an amazing player, although just a shadow of his former self. But he made the mistake of trying to keep up with the younger musicians, living at sixty as he had at twenty five. Whiskey finished him off.

Afraid of coming to the same end, Louis took care of himself. Every time he changed clothes he used Heet liniment on his chest, his back, his throat and his stomach; and took a swig of glycerine and honey frequently to clean out the pipes. Every time he had a stomach pain he ran for the Maalox, and used a lip salve made by a trombone player in Germany. He carried his trumpet mouthpiece in a back pocket, wrapped in a handkerchief. Leave it in dressing rooms and germs could get on it, bugs could crawl over it.

The divorce from Lil finally came through in 1938, and he married Alpha in Houston. In marriage, Alpha was not the same person she had been as a mistress. Every time Louis came home late, she fined him $5. She finally bowed out of the marriage in 1942, receiving a separation payment of $250 a month; and died some years later.

When Louis' *Trumpet Player's Lament* was cut from Bing Crosby's "Dr. Rhythm" movie in 1938, there were stories that the cutting was because of prejudice. Bing fought unsuccessfully to get the number restored. It wasn't a total loss; Louis recorded the same number.

In October, 1939, Louis began a long residency at the Cotton Club in Harlem. In the chorus was a dancer named Lucille Wilson; Lucille soon caught Louis' eye. He sent little gifts to her dressing room, at last asked her out for dinner. In 1942, he married Lucille; and this marriage lasted for the rest of his life.

Lucille ordered Louis' home life and traveled everywhere with him. She was also the first of his wives to adapt herself to the fact that in her husband's life his trumpet and his music came first, even before a wife. Lucille devoted herself to Louis and displayed uncommon tact. In an interview with Barbara Coleman Fox, she said: "Let's say the eye sees what it wants to see. There are all sorts of women in the entertainment field. They throw their arms around Louis. I have partial vision on purpose." Nor did she ever surprise him. "I call Louis when I am going to join him on tour."

During the war, Louis gained back all of the weight he had lost in the early 30s. Finally he started to follow a strict diet recommended by *Harper's* magazine, which required the taking each morning of a glass of Pluto Water on an empty stomach. His weight fell from 224 to 184, and he started sending the diet to any of his friends who made the mistake of expressing an interest.

During the war, Louis continued to tour with his various bands, playing many service bases. But with the end of the wary, the day of the big band seemed to be over. By 1947, Louis was playing one-nighters with a sixteen-piece band for $350 a night—$650 on Saturday nights.

Ernest Anderson wanted to put together a smaller jazz group, but he was unable to get Joe Glaser's attention. At last he got a bank draft for $1,000 and gave it to the switchboard girl to take into Glaser's office. A moment later Joe popped out, demanding to know what the check was for.

Anderson told him he'd have to come in and explain; Glaser said he could have five minutes. Max Jones quoted Anderson's reminiscences: "Well, I talked about the 350 for Louis and the whole band, and the thousand bucks, and told him I had a date on the Town Hall for a Saturday night. 'Give me Louis for the evening and leave the sixteen men behind.''

He got Louis for the thousand and added Bobby Hackett as musical director. Hackett was paid $50 for the night, Jack Teagarden, $75. Peanuts Hucko was included, and George Wettling and Sid Catlett on the drums. Wettling played the first half of the concert, Catlett the second. Sidney Bechet was also hired, but he didn't show up. Bechet claimed to be sick, but he was said to be playing at a club that night.

The Hall sold out; the concert was a tremendous success. Both the music and the notices were marvelous. Louis finished the dates already booked and never took out a big band again.

Louis always said that he did whatever Joe Glaser ordered. At the beginning they signed a ten year contract, but when the ten years were up, they never bothered making another. Louis and Joe Glaser trusted one another, respected each other, and loved each other.

So Louis Armstrong's All Stars were assembled: Jack Teagarden on trombone; Barney Bigard, clarinet; Dick Cary, piano; Arvell Shaw, string bass; Sidney Catlett, drums; and singer and dancer Velma Middleton. This was the group that was to stay together from then on.

In 1948 Louis returned to Europe for the first time since 1935, for the first International Jazz Festival in Nice, February 22-28. The festival was an immense success; the concerts were all broadcast by eighteen European stations. In 1949 Louis made the cover of *Time* magazine, on the February 21 issue. This was because he had been chosen, at long last, to be King of the Zulus for the annual Mardi Gras celebration. This was something Louis had dreamed of since he was a small boy. Enthroned on top of his float with his face painted, the King of the Zulus threw coconuts painted with Zulu heads to passersby.

At that time Louis was named an honorary citizen of New Orleans and given the keys to the city by the mayor. Many times over the years, of course, Louis was featured on the covers of music magazines, both in the United States and abroad. The *Time* cover was the first mass market magazine to so honor him. The April 15, 1966 issue of *Life*, with the first publication of the Richard Meryman interview, featured a special fold-out cover of Louis. And the July 4, 1970 issue of *Saturday Review* was also give to Louis, with a cover story on his seventieth birthday.

Louis was a happy man. In 1948 he had played a concert at Carnegie Hall; and in January, 1949, he had played at the inaugural ball for Governor-elect Adlai Stevenson of Illinois. He had crossed America so many times that even Louis lost track of his travels. Now he was about to expand those travels across the world.

11
AMBASSADOR SATCH

11

Ambassador Satch

The story of Louis Armstrong as an ambassador of jazz and as a good will representative of his native country really begins with the September 1949 trip to Europe. Joe Glaser had doubts about the commercial possibilities of the continent, doubts that were shared by most of the European promoters. England was off-limits because of the long-standing dispute between the musicians unions of Britain and the United States.

Louis was the one person who really believed in the trip from the start. The band set out for Scandinavia with a few firm bookings and a great deal of hope. Cozy Cole had replaced the ill Sid Catlett.

The flight carrying them to Stockholm was early. The pilot reported that a crowd was already gathering to welcome them in that city and suggested they stop over in Copenhagen an hour or so, to arrive on time. They did so; and when the plane at last arrived in Sweden, more than three thousand people were at the airport and a great many more outside, restrained by fences and the police from entering.

When the Americans finally made their way through the airport and into a limousine, they were accompanied by a giant parade of cars and bicycles and any other form of transport available, including a lavish float that carried a jazz band. The parade stretched nearly a mile as it made its way to a city park, where another forty thousand people, mostly young and who hadn't been able to come to the airport, waited in an amphitheater.

A local newspaper had printed the schedule of arrival; at the time, it seemed as though the whole city had turned out to greet Louis. Trumpeter Gosta Torner serenaded him with *Sleepy Time Down South* and other of Louis' favorite songs, played in his style.

Ernest Anderson, who was then with the Glaser organization, said: "We went back into Scandinavia four times that trip and must have crossed Europe five times, making jumps like Helsinki to Naples."

The European promoters had relayed a request to Glaser before the trip started that Louis not sing, fearing language problems. As he always did when presented with such nonsense, Louis ignored the requests. The fans ate up his singing as enthusiastically as they welcomed his trumpet.

Thousands stood in streets everywhere to have a glimpse of him. Concert houses were packed for two shows. In Rome, it was almost impossible to enter the theater through the crush of the crowd. Also in Rome, Anna Magnani came backstage to Louis' dressing room and found him sitting in his shorts, with his usual knotted handerkerchief on his head. His state of dress did not faze her at all..

The next day Louis had a private audience with Pop Pius XII. The Pope asked Louis if he had any children. Louis answered, ''No, Your Holiness, but we keep tryin'.'' The Pope is said to have smiled at the joke.

There were receptions, sometimes two, every single night. One morning Louis got out of bed and fell flat on his face. After that he went back to what he called his baby diet, which featured a great deal of milk, cream, malted milk and beaten eggs.

From 1950 on there was continued success for Louis with the All Stars, including regular film and television appearances. There was another immensely successful tour three years after the first ended to Europe, followed in 1953 by a short concert tour with Benny Goodman. In 1954, Louis took the band to Australia and Japan. In Australia Louis did twenty concerts in ten days, each sold out; two concerts a day. The smallest audience was twelve thousand, the biggest, twenty-six thousand.

In 1955, the All Stars once more went to Europe and then went back to Australia and on to the Far East in the spring of 1956. In May of 1956, Louis returned to England for the first time in twenty-two years. The Pan Am plane brought him to London on Thursday, May 3, to another of what was now a familiar tremendous welcome. There was a huge crowd, including many old friends from his last visit. Louis said later that it was like coming home.

From England, Louis flew to Africa on a trip that was close to his heart. The first stop was the Gold Coast, which Louis was certain was the homeland of his ancestors. Everywhere he went, he saw reminders that convinced him he was right.

On the trip to Africa, the band was accompanied by Edward R. Murrow and a CBS-Television crew, who were preparing a documentary. This program helped pay some of the expenses of the tour and after the television run was expanded and released by United Artists as a theatrical feature.

At the old Polo Grounds in Accra, Ghana, the audience numbered more than one hundred thousand people. The crowd surged forward when Louis started to play, and temporary towers that had been erected to hold the loudspeakers went down. Policemen at the front of the crowd started to use their riot sticks, but as soon as Louis saw this he put down his horn in the middle of the second number and refused to play any more.

On this African trip, Louis and Lucille found time to make a social life and see some of the sights of the various countries they visited. They saw traditional tribal dancing, and sometimes Lucille and Velma Middleton joined in. At Achimota Durbar, a festival of traditional West African dance and drum music, Louis met a woman who reminded him of his mother, Mayann.

When he left Africa, Louis claimed the experience was the second most exciting of his life. The first was joining Joe Oliver's band. Audience reaction led to world-wide publicity that was summed up by Felix Belair, a correspondent for the New York Times: "America's secret weapon is a blue note in a minor key. Right now, its most effective ambassador is a Louis (Satchmo) Armstrong. American jazz has now become a universal language. It knows no national boundaries, but everyone knows where it comes from and where to look for more."

1957 proved a noteworthy year for several reasons,

few of them enjoyable. While playing a concert before an intergrated audience in Knoxville, Tennessee, someone as a protest threw two or three sticks of dynamite into the entrance hall. No one was hurt, but the audience was close to panicking. Louis put down his trumpet and said, "O.K., folks, it's my private telephone that's just rung." With that, he started playing again, and the concert went on as scheduled.

That same year the Newport Jazz Festival had invited Louis to a special tribute on his fifty-seventh birthday. Johnny Mercer was coming to sing *Happy Birthday*, and Kid Ory, Henry Allen and Jack Teagarden were going to be there to appear with Louis. There was also talk that Ella Fitzgerald might do a set with him.

However, the Festival organizers wanted Louis to exclude Velma Middleton from the show, and to open with something other than *Indiana*, which was his standard opener at the time. Even Joe Glaser asked him to abide by the "requests," although he knew that Louis was furious. Further, no one had told Velma that she wasn't welcome.

Louis might have caved in to gentle pressure, but when people started throwing their weight around he balked. The trouble started when he failed to attend a dinner given by the Lorillards, the hosts of the Festival, before his appearance. Louis stayed in the hotel, and later explained that he never went to dinner before work. He found that dinner led to drinks and drinks destroyed music.

The organizers told Velma just before the show that she could not go on. Louis went berserk and raised complete hell. The end result was that Velma did go on, and Louis did his show his way. Johnny Mercer sang, Louis falling by habit into accompaniment.

Louis was still burning, and he blew up again when told that Ory, Teagarden and some others were waiting to join him in a finale. He exploded, saying, "No one hangs on my coattails!"

The words were injudicious and undoubtedly regretted soon after. The musicians were his friends. There were bitter words for a time, but by the next year all had been forgiven. Pops was invited back to guest with an International Band, and he augmented his All Stars with Teagarden and Bobby Hackett, both of whom he loved dearly.

1957 was also the year of Little Rock. Louis was in his hotel room in Grand Fork, Nebraska, when he idly turned on the television and saw a news report about black children being led to school on the first day of integrated education. The children had to march through a gauntlet of bitter, angry whites. Suddenly a man stepped out of line and spat in one little girl's face.

A short time later a young reporter showed up to ask Louis for an interview. He was only a boy, still in high school, but working part-time for the local newspaper. Louis gave him far more than expected, blasting the government, President Eisenhower, Governor Faubus of Arkansas, and everyone else involved. He said Eisenhower had no guts, was two-faced; Faubus was an uneducated plowboy.

The reporter rushed his story to the paper, knowing that it was dynamite. The managing editor immediately called Louis to confirm the quotes; he said he had meant every word. He was then asked if he would be willing to sign a copy of the story, and Louis agreed.

A short time later the editor showed up with the copy, and Louis signed, adding at the bottom, "Solid!" The paper put the story on the wire services, where it created

an immediate sensation. A short time later, Louis had
been invited o the White House; but when he showed
up, rather than the President, he was greeted by Presi-
dential Assistant Sherman Adams, who shook hands
and left, quickly.

The organizers of the meeting were angry, but clearly
Eisenhower had not forgiven Louis for his words. He
was taken to the Senate, where he was introduced to
Vice President Nixon, instead.

A government-sponsored tour of Russia was under
discussion. Louis refused to go through with it. Leonard
Feather cancelled a jazz package tour of the South at the
same time, and David Brubeck and Norman Granz's
Jazz at the Philharmonic scrubbed out dates in the
South and wherever local regulations mandated
segregated seating.

The University of Arkansas student government cancelled a scheduled concert with Louis over his remarks
on Little Rock. Later, in 1964, the president of the University of Alabama cancelled another engagment, saying that it wasn't because of the race situation; however,
he refused to explain the reason for the cancellation.

Louis considered himself a-political. He told Max
Jones: "I don't dive into politics, haven't voted since
I've lived in New York, ain't no use messing with something you don't know anything about. A cat came up to
me once and asked about the Big Four. I said I just hope
that combo has good time. As far as religion, I'm a Bap-
tist *and* a good friend of the Pope, and I always wear a
Jewish Star for luck."

For years Louis had suffered because a younger more
radical generation considered him a Tom. He felt that
most of the criticism was because of his stage mugging.
He was a natural performer and grew up when all black

entertainers tended to conform to the vaudeville image of blacks. He didn't say it was right, but he couldn't change himself after fifty years of living and speaking in his way.

He did contribute, generously, to black causes; but he preferred his gifts remain anonymous. After Selma, Louis said: "They would beat Jesus if he was black and marched. Maybe I'm not in the front line, but I support them with my donations. My life is my music. They would beat me on the mouth if I marched, and without my music, I wouldn't be able to blow my horn."

For that reason, Louis was most proud of his trips to Africa. He refused to return to his home town of New Orleans after the city passed an ordinance banning integrated gatherings. He did not go back until after the Federal Civil Rights Act of 1965 was passed, superceding the local laws. When the chips were down, however, Louis spoke out because he had to speak out. Perhaps he realized that he was black first, and a musician second.

That same year of 1957, after Washington, Louis toured South America. In Buenos Aires the authorities were forced to bring two large fire trucks onto the runway and turn on the hoses to break up the crowd. 1958 saw more tours, and in 1959 he returned to Europe, where the tour was interrupted when Louis collapsed in Spoleto, Italy.

News reports flashed around the world had him on his death bed. Joe Glaser was ill at the same time, and once Louis recovered a bit of spirit, he sent Joe a wire: "You have no business dying. We were put here on earth for humanitarian purposes. (Hmp). Did that come out of me? (Tee Hee). For the happiness of the world we must live longer than Methusalem."

Perhaps Louis had felt the touch of mortality before. In 1954 he had said: "I ain't leavin' this old horn nowhere, not even when I go to heaven, because I guess them angels up there are waitin' to hear old Satchmo's music too. I'm my own audience. They put a stop sign on my head, I take it right down. Me and my horn ain't never gonna stop."

Louis was back in action in a matter of weeks. That year he volunteered to take a tour, unsponsored, to Poland and Russia; but the government did nothing about it. In 1960, however, the U.S. Information Service sponsored a forty-five day concert tour of Africa. The first nine dates, in Ghana and Nigeria, were sponsored by Pepsi Cola as a promotion for five new West African bottling plants worth a reported $6,000,000. The sponsorship of the tour cost them $300,000.

At the sports ground in Ghana, all fifty thousand seats were sold out in advance. The first concert in Lagos was not so successful, Louis apparently off his form. He returned four days later, after visiting three other Nigerian towns, and a local reporter was surprised to see the difference. Now Louis played as good as he ever had.

Speaking of the tour through the Congo, Louis told Tyree Glenn: "We drew 120,000 people in the Congo. Fifty of those cats brought me to this big King. The King takes one look and yells out, 'Satchmo!' Well, I yell right back, 'Whattaya say, King?' "

The tour was supposed to continue to South Africa, but was cancelled by the government of that country for reasons unexplained. He was asked if he would have played in that segregated country, and Louis replied that he played wherever Joe Glaser told him to play. When Glaser was pressed with the same question, he ducked it by saying Louis was much too busy to play any other concerts.

The tour was interrupted at the end of the year while Louis went to Paris and filmed his part of "Paris Blues" with Paul Newman, Sidney Poitier, Joanne Woodward and Diahann Carroll. It was not a successful film. Louis then returned to the African tour, where in Freetown, Sierra Leone, Velma Middleton fell seriously ill. She was rushed to the Freetown Hospital, where she died on February 9.

The loss of Velma affected Louis deeply. They had been close associates since the All Stars were formed in 1947. But Louis accepted his grief, and continued with the tour as he knew Velma would have wanted.

People were always presenting gifts to Louis: rare records, uncommon musical instruments, cakes, booze, books, handkerchiefs by the dozen, photographs, and music and hats. He also traveled with a tape recorder, and a record player and twenty LP's. Most of them were his own music, but at the time he filmed "Hello, Dolly!", he also carried Barbara Streisand and the Beatles. That year he filled out his ballot for the Playboy poll on favorite female singer with Streisand in all three positions.

Louis had the greatest hits of his recording career in the last ten years of his life; all sold because of his singing and not his trumpet playing. The four were *Mack the Knife, Blueberry Hill, What a Wonderful World,* and *Hello, Dolly!* The last two soared to the top of record charts all over the free world.

Louis believed that music, and specifically his trumpet, controlled his destiny. He gave his horns about five years. His Selmer was always nearby—whether at home or on tour—in its open case on the table or desk, or at his feet where he could look down and see it. Every night he ran hot water through his horn, and had a series of other small daily rituals: drying and oiling, the fingering of the valves, and practice. He looked after his trumpet so it would look after him.

From 1961 on, the All Stars continued to tour the world: Africa, Australia, New Zealand, Mexico, Iceland, India, Singapore, Korea, Hawaii, Japan, Hong Kong, Formosa, East and West Germany, Czechoslovokia, Romania, Yugoslavia, Hungary, France, Holland, Scandinavia and Great Britain. In short, almost everywhere, except for Red China and Russia. The Russian trip was proposed time and again but never came through.

In 1963 there was a brief reunion with Kid Ory and Johnny St. Cyr at Disneyland; and at the end of that year, Louis recorded *Hello, Dolly!* The tune became so popular, and so identified with him, that at every concert he was forced to give it as an encore three or four times.

In 1965 Louis took six weeks off for extensive dental surgery, then flew to England. In October of that year he played his first engagement in New Orleans in twelve years. He was also given another key to the city.

Summer of 1965 was spent at the Jones Beach Marina Theater on Long Island. In 1967, pneumonia put Louis out of action for two months, but a month after recovery he flew to a series of one-nighters in Dublin, Antibes, St. Tropez and Majorca. In 1968 Louis flew to Italy for the San Remo Festival and appeared at the New Orleans Jazz Festival in June. He returned to England, then came home to enter Beth Israel Hospital in September, seriously ill. At the time he wired Tyree Glenn: "The doc says I've got very-close veins. Nothin' that a little music won't cure."

He was temporarily released from the hospital in January, 1969, but went back in for three months. In June, Louis sang at a benefit for trumpeter Louis Metcalfe. In August, he sang *Hello, Dolly!*" with Duke Ellington at the Rainbow Grill. Joe Glaser died on June 6, 1969—another of his old friends gone. Ira Mangel took over as his manager.

In 1968, a stringent diet had reduced Louis to under 140 pounds again. He bought $4,000 worth of new clothes, telling everyone that he had to stay slim. He also pressed Swiss Kriss on everyone who came near. Max Jones quoted an unnamed musician who gave the gift packet to his wife: "How did she react?"

"Can't say," replied the musician. "I didn't see her for two days and then she wasn't speaking to me."

"Hello, Dolly!" was filmed in 1968. Louis said there were twelve musicians in the scene with him, but the sound track was laid down by a sixty-piece orchestra under the direction of Lenny Hayton.

In 1970 Louis guested on many TV shows. In August, he recorded a vocal Country & Western album. The day before his birthday, July 3, he was guest of honor at a special concert at the Shrine Auditorium in Los Angeles. A week later he sang at a "Salute to Satch" night at the Newport Jazz Festival. In September he took the All Stars to Las Vegas for a two-week tour, where he worked for the first time with Pearl Bailey. After Christmas, there was another Vegas gig.

On February 10, 1971, Louis appeared on the David Frost Show with Bing Crosby, singing with Bing and playing his trumpet. Then he did the two weeks at the Empire Room of the Waldorf-Astoria, his last public appearance. The gig undoubtedly helped bring on his final illness, but the thought of not working was unthinkable.

As already told in the first chapter, Louis entered Beth Israel Hospital again on March 15th. As soon as he felt the least bit of improvement, he begged Lucille to take him home where he could once more taste the red beans and rice she had learned to cook for him, southern-style.

Lucille did take him home, where Louis celebrated a very quiet seventy-first birthday with her and with Ira Mangel. Louis talked of a concert tour he wanted to take later that year, once his legs were stronger.

Two days later, at 5:30 in the morning, Louis died peacefully in his sleep.

12
"MOVE OVER, GABRIEL"

12

"Move Over, Gabriel"

Five hundred people gathered at the Congregation Church in Corona for the funeral, while there were at least two thousand more outside. Some of the spectators were there because they grieved for Louis, but others had come only to ogle the famous. In the church, although the day was scorching hot, the only air conditioning was provided by the mourners waving cardboard fans.

Lil Hardin Armstrong was there, along with many greats from the world of show business. Moms Mabley had come with Mayor Lindsay, and there was Harold Arlen, the songwriter, Gene Krupa, Ornette Coleman, Zutty Singleton, and Count Basie's wife, Catherine.

Men who had played with Louis were there, including Arvell Shaw, Tyree Glenn, Joe Muranyi. Many more of his old friends were themselves gone. Others in the audience included Jimmy McPartland and Marian McPartland, Lee Castle, Milt Hinton, Jonah Jones, Wild Bill Davison, Monty Napolean, George Avakian, George Wein, record executive Nesuhi Ertugan. New Orleans Mayor Moon Landrieu had come.

The casket was covered with a blanket of red roses and a small red sash with the words "My Darling." Peggy Lee sang *The Lord's Prayer* so softly it was momentarily lost in the roar of a jet at nearby at LaGuardia Airport. Gospel singer Hugh Porter knelt near the coffin and sang *Just a Closer Walk With Thee*.

Blind singer Al Hibbler, guided by tenor saxoponist Walter "Foots" Thomas, sang *Nobody Knows the Trouble I've Seen* and closed with *When the Saints Go Marching In*. Ghanian musician, Little Joe Ayeshu, tried to accompany *Saints* on the kazoo, but the ushers made him stop.

The invocation was given by Franciscan father of the Reverend William J. McManus: "We know what must be taking place in your kingdom, for wherever he went in this world, there was jubilation."

Manager Ira Mangel said, "Louis was a simple man. He wanted a simple church, simple everything—no music, no sadness. He said if he had one band he would have to have all of them."

Earlier, Duke Ellington had said: "If anybody was Mr. Jazz, it was Louis Armstrong. He was the epitome of jazz and always will be. He is what I call an American standard, and an American original."

One of Louis' own statements summed up his life best: "I've never tried to prove nothing, just always wanted to give a good show. My life has been my music, it's always come first, but the music ain't nothing if you can't lay it on the public. The main thing, is to live for that, 'cause what you're there for is to please the people."

Disc jockey and close friend Fred Robbins delivered the main eulogy at the simple services: "Move over, Gabriel, here comes Satchmo." But his last words were the truest of all: "It was one hell of a show. Bye, Pops."

Afterword

On August 27, 1971, less than two months after his death and while performing at a concert in Louis' memory, Lil Hardin Armstrong collapsed and died. She had suffered from high blood pressure for many years. Newspaper stories gave her year of birth as anywhere from 1900 to 1903.

Bandmaster Peter Davis of the Waif's Home outlived his most famous pupil, dying at last in his 90s.

There were many honors and tributes, memorial concerts performed all over the world. Kid Ory led one such tribute in New Orleans, with such people as Wallace Davenport, Alvin Acorn, Sharkey Bonano and His Band, Frank Assunto and the Dukes of Dixieland, Dizzy Gillespie and Bobby Hackett. Punch Miller, himself seventy-six, played trumpet in the style of Satchmo.

Benny Carter chaired a Louis Armstrong Statue Fund, to erect a suitable memorial in New Orleans, city of his birth. Louis' first cornet from the Waif's Home is enshrined in the Jazz Museum in that city.

Of all the countless honors and tributes, however, one that might have pleased him most occurred in 1973 when the City of New York renamed the Singer Bowl in Flushing Meadow Park, near his home, the Louis Armstrong Memorial Stadium.

A FILMOGRAPHY

In a period of almost forty years, Louis Armstrong appeared in almost forty motion pictures, ranging from one-reel short subjects and animated cartoons to major musicals. Yet in that entire time, he played only one dramatic role, that of an aging jazz player in *A MAN CALLED ADAM*. In his other film appearances he played either himself or a character modeled after himself.

Black musicians appeared in many of the musicals of the 1930s through the 1950s, performing in such a way that their appearance could be cut by Southern states censors without harming the story line of the picture. In at least one instance, *DR. RHYTHM,* Louis was cut from the generally released version. Since his death, a number of films have used his recordings on the sound track; there has been no attempt to include these appearances. Louis sang "All the Time in the World" on the soundtrack of *ON HIS MAJESTY'S SECRET SERVICE,* the James Bond film in which Sean Connery was replaced for the one time only by George Lazenby.

1931 EX-FLAME, a Tiffany release; running time, 70 minutes. Directed by Victor Halperin. Screenplay by George Dranay, adapted from "East Lynne" by Mrs. Henry Woods. Cast: Neil Hamilton, Marian Nixon, Snub Pollard, Little Billy Haggerty, Louis Armstrong ᶜ His Orchestra.

RHAPSODY IN BLACK AND BLUE, Paramount. 1 reel short. Directed by Aubrey Scotto. Dressed in tiger skin costume, Louis played "Shine" and "I'll Be Glad When You're Dead You Rascal You."

1932 I'LL BE GLAD WHEN YOU'RE DEAD YOU RASCAL YOU, produced by Max Fleischer. A Betty Boop cartoon. Appearing live and in animation, Louis plays the title song, "High Society" and "Shine."

1934 COPENHAGEN KALUNDBORG (Denmark); running time, 70 minutes. A filmed revue, featuring top radio performers of the day. Louis and orchestra play, "I Cover the Waterfront," "Dinah," and "Tiger Rag."

1936 PENNIES FROM HEAVEN, Columbia; running time, 90 minutes. Produced by Emanuel Cohen. Directed by Norman Z. McLeod. Screenplay by Jo Swerling, from a story by Katherine Leslie Moore and William Rankin. Music and lyrics by

Arthur Johnson and John Burke. Musical Director, George Stoll. Cast: Bing Crosby, Madge Evans, Edith Fellows, Louis Armstrong, Donald Meek, John Galludet, William Stack, Nana Bryant, Tommy Dugan, Nydia Westman. Lionel Hampton is in the orchestra, which performs "Skeleton in the Closet."

1937 **ARTISTS AND MODELS**, Paramount; running time unknown. Produced by Lewis E. Gensler. Directed by Raoul Walsh. Screenplay by Walter De Leon and Francis Martin, from a story by Sig Herzig and Gene Thackrey. Music by Ted Koehler, Victor Young, Harold Arlen, Burton Lane, Frederick Hollander and Leo Robin. Featuring a cast of fifty-five credited performers, including Jack Benny, Ida Lupino, Richard Arlen, Gail Patrick, Ben Blue, Judy Canova, Hedda Hopper, Rube Goldberg, Martha Raye, Connie Boswell, Donald Meek, Andre Kostelanetz and his Orchestra, Louis Armstrong and his Orchestra, and The Yacht Club Boys.

EVERY DAY'S A HOLIDAY, Paramount; running time unknown. Produced by Emanuel Cohen. Directed by A. Edward Sullivan. Screenplay by Mae West. Music and lyrics by Sam Coslow, Hoagy Carmichael, Stanley Adams and Barry Grivers. Musical Director, George Stoll. Cast: Mae West, Edmund Lowe, Charles Butterworth, Charles Winninger, Walter Catlett, Lloyd Nolan, Louis Armstrong, Herman Bing, Chester Conklin, and others. Louis performed "Jubilee."

1938 DR. RHYTHM, Paramount; running time, 80
minutes. Produced by Emanuel Cohen. Directed
by Frank Tuttle. Screenplay by Jo Swerling and
Richard Connell, from "The Badge of Policeman
O'Roon," by O. Henry. Musical Director, George
Stoll. Cast: Bing Crosby, Beatrice Lillie, Andy
Devine, Laura Hope Crews, John Hamilton, Ster-
ling Holloway, Franklin Pangborn, and others.
Louis' performance of "The Trumpet Player's
Lament" was cut from the generally released
print.

GOING PLACES, Warner Brothers; running time, 85
minutes. Produced by Hal B. Wallis. Directed by
Ray Enright. Screenplay by Sig Herzig, Jerry
Wald and Maurice Lee, adapted from "The Hot-
tentot," by Victor Mapes and William Collier, Sr.
Music and lyrics by Harry Warren and Johnny
Mercer. Musical Director, Leo F. Forbstein. Cast:
Dick Powell, Anita Louise, Allen Jenkins, Ronald
Reagan, Eddie "Rochester" Anderson, Louis
Armstrong, Maxine Sullivan, and others. Louis
performed "Jeepers Creepers."

1942 "I'll Be Glad When You're Dead You Rascal
You," "Shine," "Sleepytime Down South,"
"Swingin' on Nothin'," The Soundies Corporation; running time, three or four minutes. Produced for penny arcade movie machines; not released for theatrical performances.

1943 CABIN IN THE SKY, M-G-M; running time, 98
minutes. Prodcued by Arthur Freed. Directed by
Vincente Minnelli. Screenplay by Joseph Schrank.

Musical adaptation by Roger Edens. Musical Director, Georgia Stoll. Cast: Ethel Waters, Eddie "Rochester" Anderson, Lena Horne, Louis Armstrong, Rex Ingram, Kenneth Spencer, Butterfly McQueen, Duke Ellington and his Orchestra, the Hall Johnson Choir.

1944 ATLANTIC CITY, Republic; running time, 86 minutes. Associate Producer, Albert J. Cohen. Directed by Ray McCarey. Screenplay by Doris Gilbet, Frank Gill, Jr. and George Carleton Brown from a story by Arthur Caesar. Musical Director, Walter Scharf. Cast: Constance Moore, Charley Grapewin, Jerry Colonna, Buck & Bubbles, Dorothy Dandridge, Joe Frisco, Al Shean, Paul Whiteman and his Orchestra, Louis Armstrong and His Orchestra, and others.

JAM SESSION, Columbia; runnng time, 77 minutes. Produced by Irving Briskin. Directed by Charles Barton. Screenplay by Manny Seff from a story by Harlan Ware and Patterson McNutt. Musical Director, M. W. Stoloff. Cast: Ann Miller, Charlie Barnet and his Orchestra, Alvino Rey and his Orchestra, Jan Garber and his Orchestra, Glen Gray and his Orchestra, Louis Armstrong and his Orchestra, Teddy Powell and his Orchestra, and The Pied Pipers.

1945 PILLOW TO POST, Warner Brothers; running time, 92 minutes. Produced by Alex Gottlieb. Directed by Vincent Sherman. Screenplay by Charles Hoffman from a story by Rose Simon Kohn. Musical score by Frederick Hollander. Musical Director,

Leo F. Forbstein. Cast: Ida Lupino, Sydney Greenstreet, William Prince, Stuart Erwin, Ruth Donnelly, Bobby Blake, Louis Armstrong and his Orchestra, and others.

1947 NEW ORLEANS, United Artists; running time 89 minutes. Produced by Jules Levy. Directed by Arthur Lubin. Screenplay by Elliott Paul and Dick Irving Hyland from a story by Elliott Paul and Herbert J. Biberman. Musical Director, Nat Finston. Cast: Dorothy Patrick, Arturo DeCordova, Irene Rich, Billie Holliday (in her ony feature film performance), John Alexander, Richard Hageman, Marjorie Lord, Louis Armstrong, Kid Ory, Zutty Singleton, Barney Bigard, Bud Scott, Red Callendar, Charlie Beal, Woody Herman and Meade Wux Lewis.

1948 A SONG IS BORN, RKO/Samuel Goldwyn; running time, 113 minutes. Produced by Samuel Goldwyn. Directed by Howard Hawks. Story by Thomas Monroe and Billy Wilder. Musical Directors, Emil Newman and Hugo Friedhofer. Cast: Danny Kaye, Virginia Mayo, Benny Goodman, Louis Armstrong, Charlet Barnet, Buck & Bubbles, the Gold Gate Quartet, Tommy Dorsey, Lionel Hampton, Mel Powell, Page Cavanaguh Trio, Russo & the Samba Kings, Hugh Herbert, Sidney Blackmer, Louis Bellson, and others_

COURTIN' TROUBLE, Monogram; running time, 56 minutes. Produced by Louis Grey. Directed by Ford Beebe. Story and screenplay by Ronald Davidson. Musical Director, Edward Kay. Cast:

Jimmy Wakely, Virginia Belmont, Leonard Penn, Louis Armstrong, and others.

HERE COMES THE GROOM, Paramount; running time, 113 minutes. Produced and Directed by Frank Capra. Screenplay by Virginia Van Upp, Liam O'Brien and Miles Connolly from a story by Robert Riskin and Liam O'Brien. Musical Director, Joseph J. Lilley. Cast: Bing Crosby, Jane Wyman, Franchot Tone, Alexis Smith, James Barton, Robert Keith, Anna Marie Alberghetti, H. B. Warner, Louis Armstrong, and others. Louis performs "In the Cool, Cool, Cool of the Evening."

1951 **LA BOTTA E RIPOSTA** (Italy). A series of music hall sketches, featuring among others Fernandel and Louis Armstrong.

THE STRIP, M-G-M; running time, 85 minutes. Produced by Joe Pasternak. Directed by Leslie Kardos. Screenplay by Allen Rivkin. Orchestrations by leo Arnaud and Pete Rugulo. Cast: Mickey Rooney, Sally Forrest, William Demarest, James Craig, Kay Brown, Louis Armstrong, Tommy Rettig, and others.

1952 **LA ROUTE DU BONHUER** (France/Italy). Directed by Maurice Cabro and Giorgio Simonelli. No other information available.

GLORY ALLEY, M-G-M; running time, 79 minutes. Produced by Nicholas Nayfack. Directed by Raoul Walsh. Story and screenplay by Art Cohn. Musical Director, Georgie Stoll. Cast: Ralph

Meeker, Leslie Caron, Kurt Kaszner, Gilbert Roland, John McIntire, Louis Armstrong, Jack Teagarden, Dan Seymour, and others.

1954 **THE GLEN MILLER STORY,** Universal; running time, 116 minutes. Produced by Aaron Rosenberg. Directed by Anthony Mann. Screenplay by Valentine Davis. Cast: James Stewart, June Allyson, Charles Drake, George Tobias, Henry (Harry) Morgan, Frances Langford, Louis Armstrong, Gene Krupa, Ben Pollack, The Archie Savage Dancers, The Modernaires, Marion Ross, Irving Bacon, Barton McLane and Sig Ruman.

"You Are There," CBS-Television. Louis portrayed Joe "King" Oliver.

1956 **HIGH SOCIETY,** M-G-M; running time, 107 minutes. Produced by Sol C. Siegel. Directed by Charles Walters. Screenplay by John Patrick from "The Philadelphia Story" by Philip Barry. Music adapted by Johnny Green and Saul Chaplin. Lyrics by Cole Porter. Orchestrations by Conrad Salinger and Nelson Riddle. Cast: Bing Crosby, Grace Kelly, Frank Sinatra, Celeste Holm, John Lund, Louis Calhern, Sidney Blackmer, Louis Armstrong, and others.

1957 **SATCHMO THE GREAT,** United Artists; running time, 63 minutes. Produced by Edward R. Murrow and Fred W. Friendly. Narrated by Edward R. Murrow. A documentary featuring Louis Armstrong, with Edward R. Murrow, Leonard Bernstein and W.C. Handy.

1958 JAZZ ON A SUMMER'S DAY No information available.

1959 KAERLIGHEDENS MELODI (credited by Sweden and Denmark.)
(A Girl, a Guitar and a Trumpet; also translated as The Formula of Love. These may be different films.) Running time, 87 minutes. Directed by Burt Christenson. Louis Armstrong and his Orchestra appear in a jazz cellar sequence.

THE BEAT GENERATION, M-G-M, running time, 95 minutes. Produced by Albert Zugsmith. Directed by Charles Haas. Screenplay by Richard Matheson and Lewis Meltzer. Musical Director, Albert Glasser. Cast: Steve Cochran, Mamie Van Doren, Ray Danton, Fay Spain, Louis Armstrong, Jim Mitchum, Cathy Crosby, Ray Anthony, Dick Contino, Vampira, Billy Daniels, Irish McCalla, Maxie Rosenbloom, Charles Chaplin, Jr.

THE FIVE PENNIES, Paramount; running time, 117 minutes. Produced by Jack Rose. Directed by Melville Shavelson. Screenplay by Jack Rose from a story by Robert Smith. Music scored and conducted by Leith Stevens. Cast: Danny Kaye, Barbara Bel Geddes, Louis Armstrong, Bob Crosby, Harry Guardino, Susan Gordon, Tuesday Weld, Valerie Allen and "The Pennies," Bobby Troup, Ray Anthony, Shelley Manne, Ray Daley. The life story of trumpeter Red Nichols.

THE NIGHT BEFORE THE PREMIERE (West Germany); running time, 98 minutes. Directed by

George Jacoby. Starring Marika Rokk, and featuring Louis Armstrong.

1960 LA PALOMA West Germany); running time, 100 minutes. Directed by Paul Martin. A filmed revue.

1961 AUF WIEDERSEHN (West Germany); running time, 98 minutes. Directed by Harald Philipp. No other information.

PARIS BLUES, United Artists; running time, 98 minutes. Produced by Sam Shaw. Directed by Martin Ritt. Screenplay by Jack Sher, Irene Kamp and Walter Bernstein from a story by Harold Flender, adapted by Lulla Rosenfeld. Music by Duke Ellington. Cast: Paul Newman, Joanne Woodward, Sidney Poitier, Louis Armstrong, Diahann Carroll, and others.

LOUIS ARMSTRONG AND HIS ALL-STARS, Goodyear Tire and Rubber Co.; running time, 25 minutes. Produced by Mike Bryan. A documentary.

1962 DISNEYLAND AFTER DARK, Walt Disney Productions; running time, 46 minutes. Featuring Louis Armstrong and his Orchestra, with Kid Ory and Buddy St. Cyr.

1963 "Louis Armstrong," documentary by Richard Moore; running time, 30 minutes. Produced by Ralph J. Gleason for public television station KQED.

1965 WHERE THE BOYS MEET THE GIRLS, M-G-M;

running time, 110 minutes. Produced by Sam Katzman. Directed by Alvin Ganzer. Screenplay by Robert E. Kent, adapted from "Girl Crazy" by George and Ira Gershwin. Music composed and conducted by Fred Karger. Cast: Connie Francis, Harve Presnell, Louis Armstrong, Herman's Hermits, Sam the Sham, The Pharoahs, Liberace, Sue Ann Langdon, Fred Clark, Frank Faylen, and others.

1966 A MAN CALLED ADAM, Embassy; running time, 102 minutes. Produced by Jim Waters and Ike Jones. Directed by Leo Penn. Screenplay by Lee Pine and Tina Rome. Music by Benny Carter. Cast: Sammy Davis, Jr., Louis Armstrong, Ossie Davis, Cicely Tyson, Frank Sinatra, Jr., Peter Lawford, Mel Torme, Lola Falana, Johnny Brown, and others.

1968 JAZZ THE INTIMATE ART. Running time, 53 minutes. Documentary produced by Robert Drew and Mike Jackson.

1969 HELLO, DOLLY!, 20th Century-Fox; running time, 148 minutes. Produced by Ernest Lehman. Directed by Gene Kelly. Screenplay by Ernest Lehman, adapted from "The Matchmater" by Thorton Wilder. Music scored and conducted by Lennie Hayton and Lionel Newman. Songs, music and lyrics by Jerry Herman. Orchestrations by Philip J. Long, Lennie Hayton, Joseph Lipman, Don Costa, Alexander Courage, Warren Barker, Frank Comstock and Herbert Spencer. Cast: Barbra Streisand, Walter Matthau, Michael Crawford, Louis Armstrong, Marianne McAndrew, E.J. Peaker, Tommy Tune, Fritz Feld, J. Pat O'Malley.

1970   **ANATOMY OF A PERFORMANCE;**
        TRUMPET PLAYER'S LAMENT;
        FINALE: directed by George Wein and Sidney J. Stiben. Three documentaries about Louis Armstrong's final appearance at the Newport Jazz Festival.

1971   **BLACK MUSIC IN AMERICA: FROM THEN TILL NOW.** Running time, 25 minutes. Documentary produced by the Learning Corporation of America.

A SELECTED DISCOGRAPHY

It has been estimated that Louis Armstrong cut more than twenty-five hundred sides during his long recording career, including hundreds of appearances as a back-up man for other artists. It is probably impossible to assemble a complete list of his recordings made over a period of forty-six years. What follows is a representative sampling of currently available albums.

(Abbreviations of record labels: A.F., *Archives Folkways;* Bio., *Biograph*; Bb., *Bluebird*; Col., *Columbia*; CSP, *Columbia Special Products;* Ml., *Milestone*; Voc., *Vocalion*.)

Louis Armstrong & King Oliver (1923-1924)   Ml.48017
The Louis Armstrong Story, 4 Volumes (1925-1931)

Vol. 1, with Hot 5	Col. CL-851
Vol. 2, with Hot 7	'' CL-852
Vol. 3, with Earl Hines	'' CL-853
Vol. 4, Favorites	'' CL-854
Genius, Vol. 1 (1923-1933)	2-Col. CG-30416
V.S.O.P., Vol. 1 (1931-1932)	CSP JEE-22019
Satchmo -	
Autobiography, 4 volumes	4-MCA-10006
July 4, 1900 - July 6, 1971, 2 volumes	2-RCA VPM-6044
Young Louis Armstrong with Orchestras,	
2 volumes (1932-1933)	2-BB. AXM2-5519
Ambassador Satch	CSP JCL-840
Satchmo at Symphony Hall, 2 volumes	2-MCA 4057E
The Legendary Louis Armstrong	RCA CPL-12659-E
Louis Plays Fats	CSP JCL-708
Louis Plays the Blues	Bio. C-6
Louis Plays W.C. Handy	CSP JCL-591

The following are anthologies of several bands:

Best of Dixieland	RCA ANL1-1431E

(with Turk Murphy, Muggsy Spanier, Henry "Red Allen, Bunk Johnson, Bob Scobey, Jimmy McPartland, Original Dixieland Jazz Band, etc.)

Early Viper Jive	Stash 105

(with Cab Calloway, Earl Hines, Duke Ellington, Wingy Manone, Andy Kirk, McKinney's Cotton Pickers, etc.)

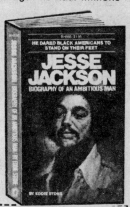

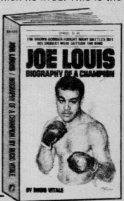